Wino in a three piece suit

Wino in a three piece suit

Vincent Seplesky

Library of Congress Control Number:		2004195229
ISBN:	Hardcover	978-1-4134-8064-1
	Softcover	978-1-4134-8063-4

This book was printed in the United States of America.

To order additional copies of this book, contact:
Xlibris Corporation
1-888-795-4274
www.Xlibris.com
Orders@Xlibris.com
27443

To my Higher Power whom I wish to call and
I am pleased to call, God

Acknowledgments

Irene, Vinny, Michael and Mary Seplesky; Ivan Mora (Cover design); Karen Jorgensen; Rubin, Isa, RJ and Ferdinand Linares; Pat and Frank Newall; Anita Darby; Frs. Murray, Ruffel and Laredo; Dorothy Acevido; Drs. Geiger, Blum and Levandusky; Nabil Attalla; Joan and Ed Neff; Dell Weeks; Peter O' Brien; Bill Swank; Marge and John Ingrussia; Joel Murov, Ann and Bernie Murray; Eileen and Ray Kopf Walker; Cita Jones; Muriel and Ernie Leckenbush; Ed Cameron; Barney L; John McDonough; John Maude; Conrad Veraguth; Betty Jurica; Joyce and John Vitkevich; Alfred Cigna; Karen, Ken and Alexa; James Mitchell; Sonia and Johnny Holmer—Mike; Gloria and Rick Porzio; Violet and Charles Vrazel; Adele and Paul Groy; Anna and Hans Weindler; Andrew Edelson, Tom, Terri Marra, Sal, Carol, Cliffzalis, Jaime, Maragni, Dr. Laura Rabin, Justine Walter Amudson.

Preface

"Joy not shared soon dies"

I might begin with I had written this book twenty-five years ago. I had it all on tape, cassette tapes, rather. I gave the tapes to a high school friend at our 25th high school reunion. Two months later she informed me that she had lost the tapes, and I had become discouraged. The friends' name was Dinky, approximately two years previous to this writing, I redid the book, with three other tapes and I decided "ok, let me go on from here."

I do volunteer work for EPRA, a Vocational Program for Recovered Alcoholics in Manhattan. I gave the second tapes to one of the staff members who said she would be good enough to transcribe the tapes for the book, in her off time. I very much trusted her, and well, needless to say the staff member was terminated, dismissed, and fired, for whatever reason. She was a very interested lady, an offspring of a Puerto-Rican mother and a father who was a combination of An African American and Native American. Anyway, I tried to do with Michaela, who was handling the transcribing of my tapes. I phoned her exactly thirty-five times, only to get her voice mail. Once she did talk to me, and said she would arrange to get the tapes back to me, she would bring them to the EPRA. That was about twenty-five previous calls, since then nothing.

I don't know how emotionally disturbed she may be from the happening, but I believed that my only recourse now is to redo the book. So, here I go for the third time and yet I still believe. What may have given me the determination to re-write the book was one day whilst listening to talk radio, they were doing a piece on Ernest Hemingway's family. It was about how his wife once threw out an entire trunk full of unpublished short stories that Hemingway had written. Not knowing what they were, or their value. Ernest was very upset, yet he decided to continue writing regardless. So, I'll take a page from his book, and call it Vincent Ernest Seplesky, in tribute. Oh! Be it these chapters would be rambling because of thoughts going from different spaces and times of my life, recollections and reflections as well. I will now consider this to hopefully be the last time this book will have to transcribe, and not only that, but be it the last time I have to go through restless days remembering my past, both the bad and good.

Chapter 1

Early years, middle years, later years. And combinations thereof. A side thought: I was going to put this in book two, but book one was never published, because of the missing tapes. I once tried to locate somebody and I contacted a tracing firm that I got from an advertisement from the radio. I sent money to the tracing firm for the use of their services after talking to one of their employees. I hadn't heard from them for several months regarding the party I wanted traced. So, I phoned them as to what was taking so long, and needless to say, their phone had been disconnected. Ironically, I had to get another tracing company to find the first. I was born in Brooklyn, New York, and it was an interesting childhood. For some reason of which I could only suspect in retrospect, my mother wasn't mentally capable of handling me. So, in hearing things bit-by-bit from relatives, they placed me with my father's parents in a small coal-mining town in Pennsylvania. The town's name was Tamaqua, nestled somewhere between Tascarora and Nescahona. I liked it in that town. My grandfather was a coal miner, and my grandmother worked very hard, and her daughter, who was my aunt, was decent to me especially guiding me and my religious education, my school studies, and picnics and other special events she would arrange for me. My aunt was unmarried and so she would remain so because she chose to care for her mother who wasn't in the best of health. She was a strong person. I was visited by my parents, who to me were "my Uncle Bill and Aunt Helen." I would only find out at the age of eight that this "aunt and uncle" were my real mother and father. My mother's thinking was a little off, so it was my father who helped me whenever they would visit from New York. I liked being around my father in particular, he would take me fishing, and swimming. I especially liked when he would bring me up to Brooklyn for summer vacation, and I liked the fact that I got to visit different parts of Brooklyn.

I did care that I was missing out on my summers in a coal-mining town that was surrounded by mountains and lakes and everything you would really love to have as enjoyments more than city streets. At the age of eight when I found out that my Uncle Bill and Aunt Helen were my real parents, my first thought was; gee, I have two mothers and two fathers. All that time I believed that my grandparents were my parents. At eight years old I made an adult decision that I was going to live in Brooklyn with my parents, (a bad move for an eight year old.) When I was with my parents I found out that my mother was constantly screaming at my father, and he would never answer her back, ever. I recall being in bed at ten o'clock listening to my mother yelling at my father. Who, by the way, I was never able to call them 'father' or 'mother' because I always called them Bill and Helen.

I was beginning to regret this adult-decision I made at the age of eight years old. Transferring to city-life from a lovely little country town. I recall how overjoyed my father was when we were driving along in the car, just me and him, and I spoke up and I said "I have decided to come live with you and Helen." My father was so excited and happy when he spoke to his wife (my mother). "Gee," "my father said, the boy has decided to come live with us, I did not have to talk him into this or speak to him about it." Now, I was living and going to school in Brooklyn, and spending my summer vacation in Tamaqua. The thing I remember about summers in Tamaqua was knocking around in old clothes playing in the dirt, swimming, climbing mountains, and trees. Then I'd go home and take a bath and I'd get dressed up in my Sunday best. No floppy old sloppy sneakers, but shoes, and how I loved to go down the street all spiffed up and listen to the high school band rehearse. The Tamaqua drum and bugle corps. You know, Tamaqua was the only town around there that had it's own pool: it was called the Bungalow, although I never found a bungalow there. We would get our swimming trunks somewhere in the woods there in the area, and just go down to the pool. When they cleaned out the pool every Monday. I recall the fire department being there with their hoses, and an empty pool and they were trying to hose out all of the slush and the slime, and the glung and the gook and all that had accumulated through the past week. Whew, was that water ever cold once they filled it up with the hydrant water and everything else that was like ice, until the sun had a chance to do warming. But we were there, a little gang of us, in that ice water, as soon as it was filled up, because it was happy times.

I recall my aunt taking me to the Lutheran church to try Baked Bean luncheon every year. This is where I would be to instead of get out of my going to school that day. My aunt worked for the Millers Dress Company in the town. It was better clothing for women; they had the bon ton where you could get off-the-rack cheaper dresses, and with a little bit more money you could get Miller's upscale dresses. My aunt did sewing alterations that were necessary for the people who purchased the dresses. What a Norman Rockwell existence it was. I look back at that with fondness, nostalgia and longing. I recall my next door neighbor Betty-Jane, my cousin Eleanor, my good friend's Buddy and Bobby, and in particular my second grade teacher Ms. Hegarty, who always thought it strange that other little children wanted to be cops and firemen. I always wanted to be a priest. I wonder at times about Ms. Hegarty, when I am donning my monk's robes without full priesthood but in the brotherhood of the Franciscan order. But that's getting ahead of the story.

I've left Tamaqua, I am in Brooklyn, NY with my parents, trying to get by with my mother's attitudes. My mother was just about five feet tall, and I don't think she weighed a hundred pounds. Those genes were the first part of my life, because I could not gain weight no matter how much I ate, I stayed what you call 'skinny.' Oh, at times in my life now how I would like to, with good health, be skinny instead of weight problems which developed, I started putting on pounds very easily. What I liked about Brooklyn was my parents would rent a cabin in the Rockaways for the summer. We would stay there, and how lovely it was to be at the beach everyday with the ocean, the water, the swimming, the sun, and the relatives, of whom, always descended upon us in the summer. My relatives loved the beach, and our little cabin where they could swim and enjoy having fun in the sun. My mother would say "where are they the rest of the year where we're back in Brooklyn away from the seashore?" I said "Mom they did not want any part of you then, because I don't think they wanted any part of you when they were at seashore. They wanted the sun, the sand, the surf, and the boardwalk fun." But that's taking inventory, mother, wherever you are. I guess on the other side of the planet Earth, I pray you are resting well. You had no choice but to be the way you were, and that is regrettable. I understand now, as it may seem, that I'm talking to my mother right now, and having sorrow for they way of life she had to lead. Rest in peace.

I am of Lithuanian heritage. My parents were both of Lithuanian heritage, my grandparents on both sides were Lithuanian, and my father understood Lithuanian very well, and he was working for consolidated Edison. He used to go to houses at times, that were owned by Lithuanians, and as he was in the kitchen, talking with the people in English, he would hear the wife say to her husband "I'll keep him busy while you go downstairs and do all the un-wiring and everything else that we put in between readings so it saves money on electricity." All of this was said in Lithuanian with my father understanding exactly what was going on in the house. What a nice man my father was, and I regret he lived with conditions that were intolerable for any person. Not realizing that someday in my life that I would pick up the same way with a marriage that my father was in, and try to live that out with all the nonsense that went on from my wife towards me. But that's further on into the story also.

Chapter 2

I went to Public School 75 and Public School 74, which got me through the eighth grade and graduation set for high school. With grades that were not satisfactory with the low ratings in arithmetic, even though my father was a super electrician, yet his son, me, was not able to put in the fuse, correctly, and I don't know to this day if I could still handle putting in a fuse. My father could rewire a house without trouble at all. High school time comes, and I went to Glover Cleveland High School. I would take the DeKalb Avenue trolley in Brooklyn up through Grandeur Avenue to school, and here was a new experience. But along with those teenage years came acne, which I called terminal acne. A lot of the redness of the boils settled on my nose, and I had the nickname of 'cherry-nose.' My mother was not for doctors, she believed in the doctor Van Dallen in Daily newspaper, who had little articles on health. She would cut those out of the paper and save those in a shoe box, meanwhile what I was saving in a shoe box, since my mother would not let me go to a doctor, were lotion, potions, and salves and creams and everything that came along from the back of a comic book, or a well-meaning person that was supposed to be the magic answer of taking away this acne. None of that worked. I spent a good portion of my high school career dealing with this 'cherry-nose' problem. Eventually my high school activities that I got involved with were pleasant enough that I got a lot of enjoyment out of the high school years, except for the fact that my friends were all taking girls to the movies, dating and all that kind of business. I could not even talk to a girl; I had trouble talking to people, because I was sure they'd be staring at my nose, and indeed they were. Every once in a while, when I thought I was getting a bit of my face cleared up and I thought I looked like the movie actor Allan Lad, that I would walk into the library in my neighborhood, and my librarian would just say "oh my goodness, you poor fellow, here's what I suggest would clear up your condition"

She'd give me something else to put in that magic shoe box of mine along with other potions! I wound up with Epson-salt and sponges on my face and all that, and I really needed to see a dermatologist, it was a deep-seeded condition.

Eventually, without my mother's permission, did I go see a dermatologist. Within one month my face was as clear as could be. But that was post-high school. I had graduated, and I just wanted to get my face looking more normal. I am recalling the story of Oscar Wilde, who had a red bulbous nose, and he was invited by a socialite for an afternoon of tea, and the socialite said to her precocious little daughter "when you meet Mr. Wilde, please do not say anything about his red nose." Sure enough the day comes, and Mr. Wilde shows up at the door, and there's that little girl staring up at his nose, and mother saying to herself 'oh don't say anything about the nose, daughter don't say anything, don't remark about the nose', and she's so sweating this out, the mother, that finally says to the little daughter "well you've met Mr. Wilde, why don't you go out and play darling." The daughter scoots out of the house, and Wilde and the socialite sit down for tea, and she pours the tea into his cup, and says to him "Mr. Wilde, do you use sugar in your nose?"

I've tried for the different sports teams in school, but was not well enough technically with sports to be accepted on any of the teams that I tried out for, including soccer and swimming, but . . . track accepted me, and I thought "gee, here I am, on the track team, heading for my school letter." Glad that I could run fast, because the bullies used to chase after me in Tamaqua, Pennsylvania, and they would also chase after me in Brooklyn, NY when I lived on Mormon Street. For some reason from the school to my house, after school a bunch of the fellas would just let me get ahead of them to run home and they could not catch me. So I would be in my house thinking "I made it again, I wasn't beat up by the bullies again today because I could run fast." I would then discover in high school that everybody else could run faster than me. As much as I would practice, I just couldn't get enough speed to be what you'd call anybody to earn the school letter. I was kept on the team by the coach because of my persistence during practice. He eventually gave me the school letter for showing up when nobody else would during certain practice sessions. I recall during Easter vacation the coach would call everyone out to the Victory Fields in Queens, I of course lived in Brooklyn and it would require me taking two trolley cars to get there, but I went everyday. A good hour and a half trip and I was the only person there. None of the other teammates showed up, not even the coach, so I just used the time to run around the track by myself hoping I would pick up speed. I came to the conclusion that was something one must have born into them, a gift if you will, to run that fast almost like a deer or something of the sort.

Meanwhile my mother's getting sicker in the head, and I just dismissed it as her being a difficult person to live with. My high school grades were exceptionally high, except for the science, Spanish, and math. Spanish, which was basically over the passing grade of 62. I would get on the paper 62 plus 3 equals 65, so at least I received a passing grade at the very least. To get ahead of the story again, here's a fellow with trouble in the sciences and mathematics, who has an appointment in West Point, where I could have been a cadet, my childhood dream, but who knows how I would have done at the academy which specialized in the sciences and mathematics. One thing I liked about West Point were the uniforms, the parades, and the music. Not the fact that, which didn't quite occur to me then, that this was an academy whom taught you to kill. I'm a church-going catholic, very much into this faith, developed a problem. Which to me at the time was needless to say, earth shaking. The hormones were racing, and I got into masturbation, which of course made me feel like the worst person in the world and the only one whom was doing this. The confessional priest would give me pennance, and it was very difficult to change. I seemed to make things so bad for myself that no priest would give me a pennance.

My friends were out with girls, having sex with them, I felt so much better than them because I wouldn't have sex until married, yet I found myself confused about masturbation. What was I going to do about the real sexual act, I would remain a virgin until marriage. Interesting reason why I decided to get married, I decided to because I wanted to know what sex was all about, what it felt like. A terrible reason to get married, now that I'm a part of church surroundings and order, I could get an annulment. Getting married to find out what sexual intercourse was like was far from being the right reason for doing so, but I've been married for half a century or more, fifty . . . fifty-four years I believe.

The story of me and Helga Hartwig, the sweetheart of Sigma Kai in high school. The prettiest girl who was the president of the honor society, she played in the school orchestra, and I was pretty sure that every boy in school asked her to senior prom. I decided I was going to ask Helga to the senior prom, and it took me two months to get the courage to do just that. To say those words, everyday on the trolley cars, I would pass Saint Allowish's Catholic Church, and I'd pray to Saint Allowish to give me the courage to ask Helga to the prom. Other than that, I very rarely spoke to Helga, except for those few greeting words, and one day, on a Friday, I went up to Helga and I said "Helga, I don't speak to you, but would you go to the senior prom with me?" Wonder of wonders, she says "I'd be delighted." What a shock, I only wanted the courage to ask Helga because I didn't know how to dance. As it turned out, I got a book by Arthur Murray, I think it was fifty cents, on How to Dance with Magic Step 1,2,3,4. I had that book to guide me to the senior prom with Helga Hartwig. End of story.

I recall on the track team how bad I was during my first race, a 440 yard relay, and I had to run 110 yards, and I was the starting runner. With a baton in my hand, the gun shot off, and everyone ran down the track except for me. I was just there on the starting line, looking at everyone running. I thought I should get with the scene, but by then everyone was so far ahead. I believe we finished last and it wasn't much of laughing matter. We ran a mile relay and I was the fourth person waiting for the baton to come around. Track fellow, where everybody else was finishing the race, and I was waiting for my man to come around for me to run my last quarter mile. Through the in-field I couldn't see where he was because of the crowd, and here comes my man chugging around the track and he hands me the baton, I had to run the one quarter mile with all of the hoots and hollers of "get a horse" and "which school are you from?" However, I received great ovation when I finally finished the race. The only race we've probably ever won was the Novices for Freshmen race. We were all juniors and seniors, and we came out first. Then of course would come the finals and the coach must have gotten a bit frightened. Who knows what would have happened, we would have walked off with the trophy; considering we weren't freshmen, and the coach told the judges that one of the other boys hurt his foot. So we wouldn't be running.

My good friend in high school was Otto Kopp, and Otto helped me through my mechanical drawing class. I took that as a cinch subject for me as a Senior, because you had to have your day filled with classes. I thought since I was a good artist, I'd be great at mechanical drawing. A big mistake. I couldn't draw four sides of a square block easily, and I copied Otto's work for the entire semester, and got by. Thank goodness that Otto sat next me. One day, I recall someone asking me a question about something on the subject, and Otto would ask what I was doing, I'd tell him I was helping the fellow with his project, which would lead to Otto saying "the blind leading the blind." Otto went on to become a professor of Geology at Tennessee University, and lives there today with his wife and children. A quick thought, since how our parents are, we may have a predisposition to being like them, and our parents may have a predisposition to be like their parents. So basically we are all victims of victims. Maybe like that little thought: there's a flea on the back of a dog biting him, and there's a flea on top of that flea biting him, and a flea on top of that flea biting him . . . add infinitive.

Interesting thought on alcoholism, which this book includes is, if you ever get around to it, is that rule number one is: if you are an active alcoholic and you continue to drink, you will die. Rule number two is: you can't change rule number one. This must be in the book. I may have mentioned it previously, but this is the third time I have written this book. The first time was 25 years ago at my high school reunion, I had tapes of my thoughts. I gave them to somebody, a classmate from the reunion, and she was going to transcribe them for me. Several weeks later I asked about the progress of the tapes, and she had told me she'd lost all the tapes. I would then spend two years rewriting the book, I gave the tapes to one of the staff members of the EPRA, a program of which I am a volunteer/consultant once a week, and she was a little bit on the monotone voice side with issues that concerned me, because her mother was Puerto Rican, and her father was an African American who had married a Native American. So, it must have been difficult for the EPRA person to handle life in particular. Here we are, they terminated her, and she had all of my tapes at her house, and

I couldn't get the tapes back from her due to the fact that she may have gone into depression. I made thirty-five phone calls to her voice mail, and no reply. So enjoy this book. If not for no other reason than out of pity for the author.

Interesting, although I was a judge on the student court in high school, and that had a bit of authority and responsibility to it, with black robes and court room scene, yet I just wanted to be an inspector. I was a marshal at one time, the kind that sits there and watches over the halls, but the inspector would come around and he'd have a badge, that is what I wanted, that silver badge, because they could go where they wanted and do what they wanted and get away with it. Primarily because of their authority. Although the judge had more authority than the inspector, because whomever the marshals would issue a ticket to, I would have to make the judgment as to what the decision would be for that particular offence. And of course, everyday I'd run to the trolley cart after school so I wouldn't get beat up or anything, because those that were in the courtroom weren't too favorable with the decisions I made. That's when I'd run faster than I ever have when I was on the track team. Meanwhile, the second World War had started, and my father went to the navy, as a new way of life. Sometimes I think he was getting away from his wife, my mother, for that life. A little problem there but I had no choice. I was to remain there at home, because of my youth. Now it becomes a little more intriguing. We had no phone in our house and a telegram came from my aunt, my father's sister in Pennsylvania, my aunt who helped raise me with my grandparents, my father's parents. It said to phone them in Pennsylvania at a certain time on a Saturday. My mother and I went to the nearest phone booth and we called, but there was a problem getting through. So, my mother just went home, while I was left there with the telephone and I thought maybe I should give it a try. I eventually got through to my aunt. My aunt said, "Don't you know your father was killed in action?"

Chapter 3

I'm balling like a baby, when I arrived home my mother started screaming at me as to why I had been out later than I was supposed to. She had a curfew for me, about nine o'clock, and it was about ten-thirty when I walked into the house. Me, having a problem, not only dealing with my father's death, apparently his destroyer at the battle of Okinawa had been hit by four kamikaze planes, and it was destroyed, and he went down with the destroyer. Which is ironic at best, but unfortunately that was the end of him. How could I explain that to my mother, not realizing that my mother already knew. The destroyer, U.S.S. Morrison's project is to defend the aircraft carriers, which were sending the missions over to the islands to destroy the Japanese. Still, when they left, they would give the pilots enough gas to go one-way with their lane, which was a bomb, actually. They would lock them into the cockpit, making sure when they look off they were going to live with the emperor forever. Side bar on this; later on my relatives, my mother's aunt and uncles told me that when my father was home, on his last leave, he mentioned to them that in his last battle, there was this image he saw of Jesus Christ, and Jesus Christ mentioned to him that this is the last battle you will survive. The next one you will not. Of course I was told this many years after the fact of my father's death. The problem now of trying to let my mother know, that my father's dead, that her husband is dead. I put so much effort into getting this into my head to tell her, tell her, tell her. Apparently I was just able to blurt it out the following day, on a Sunday, somehow. That is what happened and my mother explained that she already knew. She had gotten the telegram, and she was trying to save me the circumstances of death, so I would not be taken away from my school studies. Ironic, try to put that into some type of perspective for a screenplay, for a book which is fiction. I guess I jumped ahead of myself.

I finished high school and I had a choice of two colleges to choose from, I had received a scholarship to St. John's University, because I was fairly intelligent, with fairly good grades, a little bit better than fair, I'd say for a scholarship. I had also gotten an appointment to West Point. I decided to take the scholarship and go to school during the day, and take care of my mother at night because she was acting strange. I had no idea that my mother was suffering from mental illness at that time. Now I've got a fairly decent education in mental illness because of my studies, but who knew at this point in time that my mother was "wacky as a jay bird?!" So I was going to college, and one day I came home from school and my mother had sold all of the furniture in the apartment and decided to go live in the subway system. Me, as an immature son, decided to let the scholarship and college go, temporarily, and live in the subway system with my mother, to protect her. My mother and I lived for about one-year traveling the transit system, sleeping in Grand Central station and Penn Station.

All the time my mother was doing things which made no sense. She decided to go to Philadelphia; we got on the train and went to Philadelphia. My mother had money from the insurance of my father's rather unfortunate demise, and we'd get to Philadelphia, and I'd say "What do we do now?" and of course she'd say "Well we've seen Philadelphia, now let's go back to New York City." We would of course do just that, and she decides to go to Reding Pennsylvania. We'd go there on the train, and when we arrived I would again ask what was next and she would reply, yet again "Well, let's go back to New York City." This was a part of her behavior pattern, which is I would say, particularly paranoid bi-polar psychotic, if you will. I would however get my mother to land, somewhere in a place in Brooklyn, where we had a room in somebody's private house. This brings me onto the next adventure for myself, and mother. Possibly that should be a short chapter. The good news is I got a job, ta-da! I went to work.

Chapter 4

First job since high school, because my mother would not allow me to work, even in summer jobs, which was strange, but normal for my mother's perception of what life was about. I have to keep in mind that my mother's perception which is her reality, and that has to be true for her, but it was upsetting to me because all of my friends were getting summer jobs, and I was just kind of kicking around summer here, if I wasn't with my grandparent's in Pennsylvania. I would just kind of live in the streets, jealous over the fact that they were able to work, and I could not. One of my thoughts of work was to be a "soda jerk" at Shref's. They always looked like they were doing such wonderful things, making those ice cream sundaes and all that, in their nice little aprons and hats. The other one was to be an usher at Radio City Music Hall, because of the uniforms, and being in that atmosphere of luxury, beautiful surroundings, carpeting, and the warmth of what that had to offer.

Of course being around the Radio City Rockettes, which was one of my thoughts of life, to have a Rockette as a sweetheart. I kind of had that later on, if I might think of it at my Alcoholics Anonymous Club House. One of the members was a former Rockette who would not talk too much of her time at Radio City Music Hall, because of drinking and losing out on everything she once had. We became friendly-like, which was, friendly-like. A nice lady, I recall her husband was still drinking, and she went to get him from the bar one day, and a taxi came onto the sidewalk, and pinned her leg against a wall, which crushed her leg. Even though she did get a good lawsuit out of her accident it was still hard for her trying to live with a leg that wasn't much more than a pipe put back inside the original skin structure. She would come up to the meetings on her backside up the steps, how much she wanted sobriety. I recall that Rockette at one time used to be out in the streets with no shoes, directing traffic with a whiskey bottle in one hand. So she did well for herself, more power to her.

I got into a glamour career of sorts, starting in the mail room, but it was employment. Since this is not exactly in the order of time frame, a thought came to me. I was in a bar, I walked in on a Sunday to get a drink, and a bartender said to me, "You, you are not welcome in this bar. We don't want you here anymore, so you might as well get out now, and never come back in here again, and don't ever bring that dog in with you." What dog? I have no idea what happened in that bar on Saturday, maybe I was in a black out, and where ever did I get a dog and where did this dog of mine go? Joke: Tarzan swings from a vine up to the tree house, and says "Jane, make me a martini." She makes the martini, and he slugs it down one, two, and three. "Jane, make martini." He says and she does just that, again, he slugs it down one, two, and three again. Hands the glass to Jane and says "Jane, make more martini." She say, "Tarzan, don't you think you are drinking too much?" Tarzan says "You don't understand Jane; it's a jungle out there."

Quick thought on some of my training. A nice anecdote is the pastor who was guiding the jumping ahead of the game already, said there was a girl in the catholic school who was not doing too well, and when the sister of the class had got the despairing of her, she kept up the despairing attitude so the girl could not do to well, no matter what. So the priest says "Here's what I'll do: I'm going to teach you the meaning of hypo-static union. Most priests don't even know it, the nun may never heard of it, and it is a little complicated. It goes like this: the unique and marvelous union of two natures, the divine and human, and one divine person: Jesus Christ." After the girl finally learned it, the priest said "Now I'm going to come into your classroom, and we'll do this to impress your teacher." It went like this—He came into the classroom and he says "And today I might say something about the hypo-static union. Have any of you children ever heard of that?" The girl, who was in on this, says "Oh father, aren't you talking about the unique and marvelous union of two natures of divine and the human, and one divine person, Jesus Christ?" The priest said the nun nearly fell off the chair when she heard the girl say that. The girl could do no wrong afterwards, she went off to become a nurse, the girl did, and they are still in touch with one another to this day.

I must talk of this, I studied theology and apologetics, but to keep it simple . . . well, theology is the study of God. The apologetic is kind of explaining how our minds, human, could explain the existence of God. It might be something like scientist to God. "Well, I believe I could make a human being just like you did, God." God says, "Well, go ahead and try." The scientist says "First I take a handful of star dust." God stops him saying "Wait a minute, get your own star dust." So the kind that gets to whatever this Earth and all these things were made from, whatever the beginning was, it came from a source, that had to start with the maker of the source. That's the end of Religion 101, for now. Two thoughts about Tamaqua, and one is I went to a neighbor's yard one day.

. . . "Yards", that's what they called them. Apparently their dog had puppies, and I didn't realize that you don't play around with a female dog who's protecting her puppies, and I had gotten bit pretty bad. I recall being on the front porch, another word you don't hear much, being on the front porch. In front of the house with my cousin Eleanor, and we'd put our coins together and she sent me to get some candy. So I went several blocks to where I could get the special candies that she wanted, and for some reason, there was ice in front of the store. I slipped, and my forehead hit a fire hydrant. Boy, my head was busted open pretty good, the blood was coming down, and I could not really stop it with my handkerchief, nothing.

So, I held a handkerchief over my forehead and started running toward my house, and I ran back to where Eleanor was sitting on the porch. She saw me run by with this red handkerchief on my forehead from the blood, and thought I had brought red licorice, and was running to my own house without sharing it with her. Well, my grandmother and aunt couldn't stop the bleeding as much as they tried, and I was fearful of going to the doctor. I had of course just gotten back from the doctor recently from the dog bite, and back again?! Well, she got me there, my aunt. Dr. Jazak? What a name, a Lithuanian Jazak. He put a couple of stitches in my forehead, which by the way, are still there. Stitches removed, but little scars remain. Pass over to the present. This is Monday, September 13th. I am in Kings County Hospital Clinic, waiting for the doctor to take care of the fingernail and toenail fungus. I was walking from my house in Borough Park, Brooklyn, to the hospital here on Flatbush, which is about a four mile walk and I got lost. I asked for directions, and someone gave me the wrong directions. Going in the wrong directions, sensing something wasn't quite right, I ask another fellow for directions. He asks "Where do you wanna go?" I said, "I'm trying to get to the Kings County Hospital Clinic." He says "I have my car right down the block, come on, I'll drive you." He drove me right to the hospital. Ta-dah!

Chapter 5

A thought on passing through Greenwood Cemetery on the way to the hospital. I used to help a lady sell flowers on weekends, and I wondered what she was about. She had a third world accent, and one day she said to me she wanted to turn in all of the drug dealers in her apartment house, and she didn't know how to write, so she asked if I would write the letter to the district attorney for her. I went to her apartment, and she named everyone in the building, and their apartment numbers. After I finished writing the entire letter she said that she couldn't sign her name because she didn't know how to write. She wanted me to sign my name on the letter, is she kidding?

Sign my name to something like that to turn in every drug dealer in an apartment building? I think she wanted them out of the building so she could sell her flowers, which I don't think were "flowers", because how much money could she make out of a little stand outside of a cemetery. I notice nobody was ever stopping to buy. A thought: flowers, she may have been selling poppies. Poppies contain opium; opium is a drug in which we get morphine, heroine and methadone.

Bottom line is, I took the letter home with me, and I never mailed it to the D.A.'s office. This lady asked to get a doctor to sign a letter that he had been treating her for years for some condition that wouldn't allow her to work anymore, so that she could get government income, and I said "Oh yeah, Mr. Nice guy. I know a guy who'd do that." I thought more about it, what doctor, where? She kept asking me, and I kept putting her off until I got an idea. One day I said to her "well", of course thinking she had no money to speak of, I said "The doctor that I have said he'll do it, he'll give you the letter, but for risking his license, he wants $5,000 in cash." She said to me, "Ok, I could do that." What?! She never got the doctor's letter, and I finally said to her that the doctor wasn't taking any chances on losing his license, not ever for $5,000. Her answer to that was "Oh, it's a plot. They're out to get me." When I was talking to her, she'd tell me to turn my back because "they" might be watching from across the street, and reading my lips. Wow, who were "they"? On with my career.

I was promoted out of the mail room to the purchasing office of the company, as an office boy. I worked as an office boy until, I hate to say boy, I was a young man then, and got to be one of the assistant buyers, eventually. I worked hard, I know that I was doing not only my work; I was doing the work of my boss, who was a drinker. He kept a bottle in his desk, and he was always next door at the bar, and I was doing all of his work to protect him. And of course, I had to learn what his duties were for the company. A thought on my poor arithmetic; as they would call it, is when my father was on the destroyer I wrote him a letter, and I told him about the special test we had in arithmetic, and you could imagine what I got on the test. I spoke of other things in this letter, and then later on at the very bottom I said, "P.S. I got a 95!" In his return letter to me, it spoke of different things, too bad about me with that arithmetic test. He put down other areas of his destroyer life that he was on, and eventually at the very bottom he says "Congratulations on your 95."

Interestingly, when my mother and I were staying at the Brooklyn East 15th street house, with the Conselyeas, Frances Conselyea was a bit of a run-around, I might say, and her daughter, very attractive girl, would befriend me. We'd be sitting downstairs while mama was upstairs, Delores mother, would be upstairs entertaining one man or another. I recall the day when I was sitting downstairs and in comes Frances Conslyea she said to me "Let's go upstairs", and I notice that she was drunk, and then she comes to the little balcony from the upstairs, in kind of a sexy nightgown and she waits for me to come upstairs to be with her.

So, I went upstairs because I figured she was going to fall over the little balcony rail down to the bottom, her being drunk and all. Once I get upstairs to where she was, she grabs a hold of me, and takes me into her bedroom. It was like something out of a movie scene, where I'm saying to her, you know sounding a bit like Cary Grant, "Frances, I said to think of my mother upstairs, your daughter downstairs, you know, and we can't be in the bedroom", she insisted on pulling me into that bedroom however. I believe the film Graduate, and I was able to move away from that scene at that time, from that lady.

Chapter 6

Well, I did fairly well in high school in just about all the areas, and eventually I got a scholarship to St. John's University in Brooklyn, NY, at that time, and also an appointment to West Point Military Academy; my childhood dream. I thought to myself, I will not go to West Point because my mother was starting to behave peculiarly, and I might stay here in Brooklyn and take care of my mother and I'd be able to go to college at the same time. Although it was veterans' time for school and so, and although they accepted me at St. John's, I had classes at something like 9 am, and another one at 7 pm. I managed well enough. I was still taking care of my mother the best I could, and I was on the dean's honor list, which was exceptional. When my mother had sold all the furniture in the apartment and decided she wanted to live in the subway system we didn't have much of anything, of course. We ate at places like Needicks, and we had the absolute minimum of everything. She wouldn't go into any type of settled apartment dwelling, or rooming house, because she was paranoid.

My mother always thought people were out to kill her, now I know paranoia, at the time I just thought it was odd behavior and I was there to protect her somehow. We were getting nowhere, a train to Philadelphia for what? The same instance occurred, we arrived and suddenly she wanted to go back. We went to Reading, Pennsylvania, we got there and she wanted to go back. That was just a little example of what her behavior was like. What a great day it was when I was able to get her to land, somewhere in that 15th Street house with the Conselyea family. Somehow I was able to complete college, and get onto the job market and begin a career. A career in what was known as the glamour field; the super liners crossing over to Europe and back, with all the celebrities and politicians who travel on our vessels.

I may have never gotten over my celebrity admiration nature, although it isn't the worst thing in the world. When this book is a best-seller, and I'm on the talk show circuit, being wined and dined by the people who now consider me a celebrity, I'll try to remember when I was one of the "little people." So much for the irony, sarcasm, or whatever the previous was, but let me get on with what the book in my memoirs is about. When I tried to let my "boss" know what was going on, he would always tell me "they couldn't do anything to me. The ones that have the power are the ones whom I came into this firm with in the beginning. So, they'd watch out for me." Well, they were not watching out for him, because one day they told him that they would no longer require his services, and that I, Mr. Seplesky, would be the new in-charge person. That was my gateway to a new way of life, that I should have enjoyed if everything else was equal in my life. How to handle people, places and things, but immaturity in my past experiences, which I believe you never overcome your early experiences, you only compensate for them for the rest of your life. Dr. Freud, where are you?

In fact I think an interesting Freudian slip, so much of my mother's thoughts is that this Freudian slip might be, if it's not one thing, it's a mother. Or possibly I was just being a good son. Still caring for his mother's welfare, whether she wanted it or not, or was able to do anything with it or not. An anecdote of when I was with my mother on 61st Street, Brooklyn, working for the Pine family as a housekeeper/babysitter, I was the Saturday night babysitter, because my mother was not up to housekeeping or anything else for that matter. I went to a dance and I met this very attractive girl. Margie by name, Margie Fitzgerald. I asked her to dance, and as we were dancing, she says to me "You sound something like Henry Fonda." I guess my voice is like his if I lower it and talk slower, and I said to her "Well I guess I should, I'm his nephew." Well, what an opportunity that was to be with a pretty girl, but I didn't realize what it would turn into. I told her I was visiting my uncle in the city, and I was from Nebraska, and I would be going back shortly. She invited me over for the Thanksgiving weekend at her family's house, and I had to spend four days talking like Henry Fonda, and making sure my voice was always something like his. What big lies they were, about my background, and Nebraska, I even changed my name to Ken. I had Thanksgiving with my mother living in a basement of a house taking care of a family, we had a turkey dinner, my mother and I, but the turkey I had I left in the backyard because it wouldn't fit in the refrigerator. Of course on Thanksgiving day, every cat in the neighborhood had their piece of turkey, which I cut away most of it, and my mother and I had what was left. Then I traveled over to the Fitzgerald compound, if you will, and then spent the holiday with the family. They were of course, believing I was the nephew, at the dinner table, and the little daughter of the Fitzgerald's says "You know someone famous", and of course the parents, you know, jumped upon the girl like "Oh it doesn't matter famous or not, we like Ken because he's Ken." Haha.

I left at the end of the week, and I said to Margie "Let us go out on New Year's Eve, I will be back in the city for that holiday weekend. And I'll say right now, Margie, if you're reading this book, don't keep waiting for me, because Ken is not returning to New York anymore, or rather he's not returning period. There was no Ken, only Vincent, he with an inferiority complex, I guess if you'd wish to call it that. Maybe not an inferiority complex. In some respects I really was. I was kind of skinny, I was awkward, and I wasn't able to speak with people very easily, I call that "inferior." Technically it was just a belated adolescence.

Chapter 7

I decided to get married to find out what sex is about, and that was it. No knowledge or care about love, children, and other areas of a married state. And I chose a attractive girl but she only had one useful arm. Apparently as a child she developed dipheria, and the hand was left clenched, and the surgeons tried to unclench it with an operation to loosen the tendons or whatever, and they over did it, so the fingers were back, basically it wasn't very useful. And we had four children. Vincent Jr. first, Susan, second, Michael, third, and Mary-Elizabeth, fourth. There was one son, Steven during this time, that did not live past the baptismal ceremony. And since I had a new position in the company, Junior Executive status, I had all the fringe benefits that went along with that responsibility. I purchased a little estate in Pearl River, NY, in Rockland County, which I used to call Pearl River Up the Creek, because of the deep unsettled unhappy marriage. It was a picture postcard place with a private lake in front and swimming pool in back, and eight 60-foot pine trees in front, two car garage, a couple of drive ways, un-housed land next to me, (wooded land). It sure had been an ideal. I was now able to eat and drink in all of the upper-class restaurants, bars in the city of New York, take as many people as I wanted, as many times as I wanted, and it was never any cost to me. I'm a Lithuanian ancestry, and that goes back to my lineage, and my wife was Polish. And it was a bit of a mistake because it was like I married my mother.

Continuing on that art studio. Basically, it was an interesting enterprise for me, but not for the money. Although I got very good fees for my work, I was on an ego-trip, having my name on a painting that I had done. And the studio was also a good hideout for me, because I would use it as a drinking place. I think I had more alcohol in the place than paint. Now that I had all that responsibility and I wanted more time for drinking, I almost computerized any of the work that I was directly responsible for, so that by the time I had gotten into the office at 9am, I was technically finished with my work at 10:30am. The problem with marriage was that my wife insisted on her role of handling the children, which is giving a person complete freedom. The more I studied child psychology, the more I learned that children need direction and a certain amount of discipline, it may not have to be physical, but a matter of letting a child know that they cannot do what they wish to do all times. I have one example. I would be sitting in the living room and one of the children would be painting in a painting book and I was saying "you know, that's why we have a playroom. Why don't you go into the playroom because you may spill that rhetoric king on the rug." And the child would immediately go running to her mother, which was my wife, and start crying. Well the wife would start in on me "what have you said to that child"? You are impeding their maturation". I wonder if she knew what "impeding maturation" was? Probably read it somewhere in one of the magazines but then the wife would go away, and the child would come back and continue painting and turn to me and stick out a tongue. Example two, I would have new bikes for the children. I would be coming in my car, and the bikes would be laying on the driveway. And I would explain to the children that's why we have storage space for bikes, they don't belong laying here in the driveway. Of course they would go running to their mother. The mother would come running to me and I get some more of that ridiculous nonsense.

I, of course, would have clenched-fist attitude, white knuckles. I found out that if I went to the bar. We had in the house, and had a stiff belt of alcohol, I would relax. And that kind of became the way of handling the marriage, just use the alcohol and let things go as they are going. Of course, in the wrong direction, and I was going in the wrong direction also with the alcohol. I believe leading me onto active alcoholism down the line, I kind of had the same problem with my mother, since she was difficult to be around. I found out that if I had some whisky in me before I made the visit, it was easier for me to sit there in kind of a stupor and listen to her carry on about how terrible I was. And yet being the only one that she would allow near her to see that she was taken care of as far as dining out, and the essentials of her life. To take my mother into a restaurant was odd, because people stared. My mother, for whatever reason, had all the hair removed from her head. She was bald. And she removed all her eyebrows, pluck by pluck. And was dressed kind of raggedly; she was kind of a bag-lady type person,. And yet we'd walk into one of these classy restaurants with everybody looking at us, and get by, somehow. Of course, the few drinks that I had would help me to not be too upset by the people staring. An interesting thought on portrait painting. It's not too difficult to have a likeness of somebody if they are attractive. The secret is to get an unattractive person to look attractive and still have resemblance to the person. In fact what I did is, and this is ego again, I got a private art teacher to help me with my portraits that I might become even more proficient. And I would go to her house on a Sunday afternoon; I'm talking many years back, when it was three dollars per lesson for one hour's time. It was her, her husband, and two children. And of course, she would make a Manhattan for me before each lesson. And eventually it was two Manhattans; lesson times were shorter, than three Manhattans and lessons became even shorter. But she taught me one thing important, keep on with lights against dark's in your shadings, and keep the portrait's face moving with not much concentration on one part of the face, go part ear, part eye, part nose, and keep on some of the hair, possibly some of the neck, and keeps it interesting. And eventually voila, there is the resemblance. Oddly enough, my wife could not understand how I'd have art lessons on a Sunday. I would leave sober and come back staggering. I had made portraits of my children and one of my daughters was so well done that the art teacher used her connection with the World's Fair, to get it on display at the Hall of Education. In fact she said she could get me work at the Worlds' Fair as a quick sketch portrait artists, where I would make considerable money, but it would mean leaving the career I was building. I also had taken my daughter twice to that World's Fair with the family, but I was so interested in finding out where the drinks were that we got to the Hall of Education, so she could at least stand there while visitors were admiring the work of the cute little girl whose picture was hanging on the wall. Sad to say in progression of my alcoholism I was using the portraits to get some attention for myself. I would take a photograph and use that as my subject for the lesson on Sunday, and the teacher would do most of the work. She would do 99% of the work and I would put my name on the bottom of it. I had some kind of rationalization that I would eventually wind up doing portraits of people in bars for drinks. It was a sad time to come to but down the line somewhere they'd get a portrait worth $200.00, I would be satisfied with occupying a cheap shot of whisky. I recall working on one photograph of somebody's two children, and they were Caucasian and it was done rather well. And on a Saturday night while I was drinking at my apartment, I would touch it up here and there. And I didn't know how much touching-up I was doing because I had returned it to that bar at 1 o'clock on Sunday, and this was Saturday night. I went to sleep and when I woke up I looked at the painting, and they looked like Negroes, not Caucasian. I had to, within several hours turned them back into Caucasian and returned to the person at the bar at 1 o'clock on Sunday in order to get my few free drinks. I considered the life I was living was like a millionaire. I didn't have the million dollars, but I was living like I did. Where is the real difference? One of the wealthy people I know said to me, that if you could take a twenty dollar bill out of your pocket and spend it on whatever you want at that time, you are as wealthy as me. And I'm beginning to understand that, because no matter how many houses you own, you can only sit in one chair in one room, at one time. I would say I had my share of challenges. I was not only trying to take care of my wife and children, but also my mother and also a very responsible position in the company, and still be able to get a drink whenever I needed alcohol. Which the time between drinks, when I needed drinks, were getting shorter and shorter. I would travel into New York with a car pool of four other men, and I knew from the moment I left that house, I had to be at my destination in Manhattan to drink within one hour's time, or I would visibly start to shake and get all the symptoms of detoxification. So I had my very last drink by the time the car pool arrived to pick me up so I would just pray that there wouldn't be any traffic congestion to hold up the one hours drive. I can recall, needing a drink at about five am, nothing left in my house, or in my car where I had bottles hidden in glove compartments, in the trunk, under the seats, and they were all empty, I would start to drive around Rockland County, hopefully finding a delicatessen or some store open that might sell me beer, which had alcohol in it, which would keep me settled. I must have went to 10 towns, without one store being open. By the time I was ready to give up, it was 8 am, and the liquor stores were now open. And I said, "Who wants beer? Let me get my Muscatel Wine." A happy man at that time. Of course I was a member of the New York Athletic Club, and a Downtown Athletic Club; two very prestigious places to entertain others and yourself. My lunch hour could be at either place, or any other of the upscale clubs.

I prefer those places just to "show off," it showed how powerful I had become in the business world, where I might invite somebody to lunch and take them to the New York Athletic Club, overlooking Central Park, or the Downtown Athletic Club overlooking New York Harbor. I think it strange that none of the men in the car pool ever said anything about my whisky breath, or my Muscatel breath, because I must have smelt like a distillery in that car with the windows closed. But they were all executives with their own little estates and all that, maybe they were just being polite. I recall even on the day that I was to drive, I drunk as much in the morning, drunk as much during the day, and after work, before we started our drive back to Pearl River from Manhattan. In one incident in particular, I recall, there was one hill going down on the way to Rockland County on Palisades Parkway that I fell asleep at the wheel. And when I got to the bottom and woke up, I was a little shook up that I had been sleeping, and I kind of cautiously looked around to see what the others maybe thinking or saying or whatever, and they were all sleeping too. A break at that point for me. And for them, I might add, because there could have been a deadly collision if I hit anybody or anything on the way down while I was sleeping. I recall I saved a woman from a rape one day. I changed my mind. I recall an incident I'll share, of trying to get a drink, because I hadn't nothing available to drink one morning, and there was a blizzard. It had drifts up to the roofs of the houses around me, and I knew I could not last a day without my wine, so I told my wife I was going into work. And you can get into New York City by train from Pearl River, the train goes to Hoboken, New Jersey, and then you take the ferry across to Manhattan Island. A bit complicated, but my wife said "are you out of your mind, going to work today?" and I said "Well, they need me." Haha, they need me. I needed a drink and I could not say to the wife "I'm gonna go to the liquor store or I'm just gonna go out today", because she would have really thought I was insane. So I walked from my house into town into the train station through the deep snow and the train was one hour late in arriving and on the way to Hoboken, New Jersey, it was a seven hour train ride. And then I took the ferry to Manhattan, got myself the much-needed drink, and went to my office, and found that they were closed because of snow conditions. Now the fun begins: I phoned by wife and I said "I will not be home tonight because of the bad snow. I will stay at your mother's house in Brooklyn". This is before, of course, they sold the house and moved up to where we were in Pearl River. And my wife says, "get home". I don't know why she wanted me home, because it was just the nagging and everything else, the nonsense, that would go on around that household of mine, so she said "the buses might be running." Of course, I was calling from the train station in Hoboken, New Jersey. So I took the ferry to Manhattan, and the subway up to the George Washington Bridge, which was about a 45-minute ride, and no buses were running. I called my wife back and said, "no buses are running, Can't get home". She says, "You get home, go take that train". All the way back on the subway to the Hoboken Station that I had taken across now. No trains running now. I called my wife, and she says "well, you get home. Try the bus". I went all the way up to the bus depot, and the buses are not running. Well, whether my wife liked it or not, I stayed at her mother's house that night, and I don't know who she was going to nag because I was no longer there. I am writing this book as an admitted alcoholic, and in the 12 step Program of AA they say that once you are an alcoholic, you are always an alcoholic you don't get to drink normal again. It is like a cucumber becoming a pickle, it will never become a cucumber again. And I know where I crossed that invisible line they talk about. I was driving into Manhattan by myself, and on the Palisades Parkway I got all the symptoms of a heart attack, when I was sweating, I was shaking, my heart was pounding, and I did not know at that time that I was detoxing from the alcohol. So the first thing I did was pull over to the side of the road, and get rid of all the empty bottles and half filled bottles, and everything that were in the glove compartment, under the seats and the trunk. I figured if they were going to find me dead, they weren't to find the bottles on me. However, I made it into Manhattan with all those conditions and got myself a drink in a bar, and they all disappeared. And I knew from that moment on, I needed alcohol to save me from those symptoms.

I would wake up at 5am, go into the woods and throw up, so my wife wouldn't hear me. I was only about 100 yards from the house. I don't understand how she could not have heard me because most of Pearl River must have heard—you cannot throw up silently. Then I'd prepare for work with a quart of muskatel, meet the car pool and we'd drive into NYC, arriving about 8 am. I would go into a cheap bar downtown. People knew me so I secretly entered by walking sideways through an alley between 2 big buildings, go through an empty lot and climb up the fire escape to the kitchen of the bar. Sitting down on on the far end end of the bar so passersby might not see me. I would drink from 8 until 9:30 then go to my office. I could get my days work done by about 10:30 and the rest of the time was for "fun games." I would then go out for my coffee break and drink wine until about 11 o'clock. I would buy bottle of wine, go into a telephone booth and after looking around to see if I knew anyone, would take the cap off the bottle and chug-a-lug the wine, leaving the empty bottle on the seat. I was like the Clan Kent of downtown NY. I would then go to my studio and drink wine until noon, then to a cheap white rose bar and drink until about 1:30, then back to the art studio until 3 where I'd soon go on my coffee break and perform my "superman" act again. Finally, I headed back to my office and wait until 5.

If I had an appointment with somebody I would dine on their expense account, or go to my own watering holes which would be another, say hour and a half of drinking. I don't know if you'd call Waldorf Astoria a watering hole, but these are some of the places that I did my drinking. When I would go back to the same bar I started off in that morning, with the same drill, and I'd drink until six, when all the car pool met together to drive home. I would get home at about 7 pm, and drink until I became unconscious. I like to say that in Pearl River, New York, where I lived, on Christmas Eve you could always expect two visitors: one was Santa Clause, and the other was the Pearl River Police Department because my wife was upset with my drinking. Although I was not misbehaving, she did not care for me being drunk on Christmas Eve. Well thankfully, Mrs. Seplesky, I didn't either. I had no choice at that time: I was an alcoholic feeding my disease. December was party time in my career, I was invited to one or two parties everyday from December 1st to January 1st, and I tried not to miss any of them. I know some drinkers become angry and I was one that just became extra good humored about the fact I was feeling so nice with the alcohol in me. Nice anecdote on Pearl River. I got home from work one night, and there was heavy snow, and I had a long driveway. I went out with my shovel to get rid of this snow, and I said "I would give anything to have someone shovel this snow for me", soon as I said that there was a fellow coming down the main road with a tractor and plow. He stops and says "could I help you", and I said "you could plow out my driveway, if you please", and he said "sure", and I went inside and I kept on drinking while he did the plowing. When he finished, I went outside to pay him, and he says "oh no, I do one good deed a day, and this is my good deed", and he left. You know, I never saw that fellow before that night, and I never saw him after that night. So go figure on answered requests out loud. Beautiful. I recall taking my art teacher to the New York Athletic Club one night. She met me after work, she was now working at Gimbo's as their artist, and I recall her getting so drunk that she was throwing the basket of rolls all over the dining room. Interesting lady, she insisted that she drive me home at night after 5 pm. She had her car in the city, and it was a nice break to have that ride to my house by my art teacher.

How I Met Jean: The Story of Jean

She was a Kim Novak double. I went to the Cat Show in New York City. I was sold tickets to a dance. I put the tickets in my pocket and forgot about them. I was drunk as usual in Manhattan and the tickets were in my pocket. I decided to go to the Gathering. When I arrived, I noticed this Jean girl playing cards with a group of men. I said to myself, "I am going to play cards with her." I pulled up a chair and sat next to her and said, "May I play with you?" By the end of the evening I had her phone number. I called her and made a date. I was somewhat shocked at her apartment. She had 17 cats and one litter box. Cat crap and urine were everywhere. What a stench. If she did not look like Kim Novak I would have left.

As the months went by, I understand that she was a mental case with leukemia and an enlarged spleen and a dropped kidney. She did not wish to leave the house.

Eventually, her mother found out I was married and threatened to expose me to both the business and my wife. I met with Jean's mother the next morning in a bar and made satisfied that I was getting a divorce and the mother decided to approve once I showed her the divorce papers. Meanwhile, I am getting Jean's mother drunker and drunker. Then began my romance with Jean. This contributed to my alcoholism because of my guilt.

Chapter 8

I was almost trying to get caught subconsciously, I recall making arrangements for Jean and her father to dine with me at one of the upscale clubs, where most people knew me. With Jean's attitudes, she cancelled out, but I took her father, and that was okay because me and the father were ok dining together. The two of us, just two men. However, once I made arrangements for her father to dine with me aboard one if the super liners, which is very difficult arrangement to make because it is basically for the organizations that were helping our company. When I got there, of course Jean cancelled out again, it was just me, and her father. I got to the entrance, gave my name, and it was not on the list of people to enter the dining area. I thought fast, I said "Well possibly you're confused, let me check that out". I found a name there that looked similar to Seplesky, and I said. "Here you are, you just didn't get the right pronunciation". They were very apologetic and brought the two of us to the dining area, and we were having a sumptuous meal. Well about half an hour later, the Maitre D' comes over and says, "Mr. Seplesky, we regret to say that the correct party is here for this table", embarrassing moments in my adventures of pursuing the opposite sex. However, Jean's father was an easygoing fellow, and he understood and I was a very good friends with him. I believed it's what helped with my drinking because of the guilt I felt in trying to have two lives.

Sometimes I think if you wish harm on somebody, don't go for physical harm, but wish them to have a wife and mistress at the same time. Eventually Jean decided she would no longer be dating me because she didn't want to have fights with her mother whenever she returned from a date with me, so I well imagine there must've been a lot of commotion going on in the household under the circumstances that her precious daughter was involved in. As I can look back on it objectively, I believe her mother was truly right in her thoughts about the situation. In retrospect, Jean may be in some type of mental facility because she had told me during our relationship that she believes the happiest people are in institutions, so possibly she may have been in that condition before she had a relationship with me. A thought on Levittown—I was very friendly with my neighbors. He had been a stockcar driver in the racing community, and he was also the service manager of a Chevrolet Oldsmobile agency. In fact when my car had transmission trouble on a Sunday, he said he knows of a place where there is the exact car as mine that has a good transmission.

We went to the place, so I had a good one. We sold the old car that we bought as junk. Right about that time, there was a film in the movies houses entitled "A Place in the Sun" with Montgomery Clift and Elizabeth Taylor and I was kind of a Montgomery Clift type. The story was that as a man visiting his rich relatives in their mansion, he falls in love with Elizabeth Taylor. Hence my neighbor and I were driving along the Gold Coast of Long Island, and as we're going past one estate after another, I said to him, "One of my fantasies is to drive up to the front door of one of these mansions or estates and to tell the parents that I am here to take your daughter out for the evening". My neighbor by the name of Frank Lezack said to me, "If that's what you would like. I used to date somebody from one of these estates, and I'll arrange for you to go out with her". Of course he knew them from his celebrity as a stock car racer and teaching the wife of one of the wealthy people to drive a car. We got back to his house, and he phoned Kollner and arranged for me to go out with his wife's sister who's name was Helen.

When I made the date that we were going to have, the time all settled, I said "And your address"? And she said "Oh basically don't be concerned with the address, just drive along Old Guinea Road and our name is on the drive before you get to the house; for me that was class. Here I was, Montgomery Clift. "A Place in the Sun", and they lived in Old Westbury Long Island in New York State, which was about the wealthiest of all the towns in Long Island-neighbors such as the Whitneys with the horse farm, etc. I was there, I had made it. So I drove up the blue stone driveway up to this fabulous house and there I was talking with Jack Kollner about taking his sister-in-law out for the evening. We had a lovely time. Basically I took her out to a nightclub called San Su San, and it was interesting because apparently she knew the place well enough to have all of the band members come over and talk to us at one time or another, Jack Kollner said, "I have a cousin who is going to be staying with us for a while, a lovely girl". "You might want to take her out for the evening". And that eventually happened also. I took out the Kollner cousin.

That was the end of that fantasy, it all came true. I did not care too much for being around the rich because I had my own ideals of what I should be getting about in life, not hanging onto the coattails of the super rich. Where the Kollner family make money was they owned county fair pork products and it was one of the most famous products going at that time. In fact supermarkets carried that product, and there was a Kollner Square in Jamaica Long Island, which was their entire plant for making the product. (with a little sidebar on that). I was on a date with another girl and we were driving alongside the plant, which took an entire block, and I mused out loud, I said, "Boy this brings back memories" and the girl said to me, "Why? Did you work there?" And I just nonchalantly said, "Work there? I nearly owned it". Well I went and married this Polish girl by the name of Irene, who was not able to understand that one of the worst forms of child abuse is excessive permissiveness. (Say that fast 3 times-excessive permissiveness).

When we married there was nobody from my side that came, everyone was her relatives. The only people that came were my grandmother and my aunt and her new husband from the coal mining town and I made arrangements for them to stay at a hotel after the wedding. Off we went to Miami Beach for our honeymoon. I had contacts where I could get an apartment which the company that I worked for at that time had an apartment there on Indian River on Miami Beach which they kept for entertaining purposes, and I was given that for my honeymoon including maid service and a kitchen for any type of light cooking as we wished to do. There was absolutely no charge for this gift. However, with all the money I took from the wedding, for the honeymoon purposes, we still came back with about 8 cents left partly due to the fact that there was car trouble and I was taken over by a scam artist service station on the road down south, of course having New York plates, they got away with it. The fellow that came to fix the car did not fix the problem, so when I was in the car, if I ever slowed down, it would take 15 minutes to get it up to a decent speed so I kept it up well over 60 mph through these small towns in the south. I was fortunate, I was never accosted by the police.

Limits there I'm sure never reached 60 mph. But we got down there, and it was a decent honeymoon I'll say. Since there was really no real money left on the way back to New York, we slept in the car and ate Stuckey's dates. It was difficult living in Levittown with my mother's condition of paranoia, psychosis, etc. We eventually left the Levittown house and moved in with her family in Brooklyn New York, taking my mother along which was decent of the in-laws to give my mother a room in their house which had extra bedrooms. The bottom line of all that is eventually my mother was put in a state mental institution and I was appointed guardian by the court system. Then began another section of my life where I went to visit my mother every Sunday for about 2 years and it was not pleasant to spend an hour or two in an asylum, which it was, and my mother was always fearful of her life. My wife never came with me to the institution. Frankly, neither did my mothers brothers and sisters. I told them about the predicament of their sister, and yet they would not come to the asylum. One sister claimed that she would be saying something like "Crazy, go nuts". Why what were they in there; they were crazy if you want to keep it simple. By the way, that was one of the sisters that died of alcoholism. I became friends with my mother's psychiatrist at the institution and I used to drive the psychiatrist home after the visits and I was able to get my mother a weekend pass through the psychiatrist,

I took my mother out and got her a place on the Jersey shore. It was a mistake. She remained in her room and would not even come out for meals that were prepared for her by this lovely family. Now I had a bigger project for myself to get down to the Jersey shore every couple of weeks to visit my mother.

Through all this my career had been advancing, and eventually I was in charge of the department as a Junior Executive making all types of money. That is when I got the little estate in Pearl River NY it may have been mentioned before but worthwhile for it to be on these pages again with a private lake in front, a pool in the back, etc. Living the life of a millionaire even though I was not that wealthy, but I was in with the wealthy crowd. In one sense I was living life in the fast lane with the jet set, at least in Manhattan. At home I was being downed by the miserable conditions of a dysfunctional family.

The family in Southern Jersey could not cope with my mother and they asked if I could find another location, which I did. I found two elderly sisters who were willing to have my mother live in their house. It was easier to visit my mother at that location, and I did so twice a week on Saturday morning and Wednesday evening-bringing her food, taking her out for dining, and seeing that she was staying alive. In the new location, she would not come out of her room in the lovely apartment in the lovely house. It was difficult visiting my mother because she had an attitude, which made me very uncomfortable. What I would do is I would bring a bottle of wine with me for ostensibly for her. And drink it during the visit so it kept me somewhat in a calmer area of visitation. What I was doing right along the line since I had a predisposition for alcoholism was setting the fuse closer and closer to the point where it would explode one day. The two sisters could not cope with my mother and asked if I could find another space for her, which I did. This was a cabin in a resort section of Spring Valley NY, basically still in my area where visiting was still more convenient. She would not come out of her room in the 3 room cabin, and relied on me for the food, etc, to keep her going on planet Earth. These people standing on the food line at the Salvation Army as they're going past the tables with food, they passed a bowl of apples with a sign next to it that says: "Take only one apple, God is watching". Further down the line is a tray of sandwiches, and the sign next the sandwiches says: "Take as many sandwiches as you want, God is watching the apples".

A thought of the background with Jim Wheadon, other than taking me out to test his 22 rifle with the junk car, he and his sister used to take me horseback riding in Canarsie NY, I was skinny but I had Dungarees and a flannel shirt, red checked and I felt like real cowboy when I was on that horse. There was Canarsie Bay where you could ride your horse along the sand for several miles, but to get to that bay, there was a chain linked fence and it was maybe a mile ride to go around that fence to get to the water, but if you took that horse under a bridge by the fence, you would be by the bay waters immediately. It was something to get that horse walking along the bottom of that stream with my feet practically up by the horse's ears to keep myself from getting wet, but it could be done. And I did it. Also there was a section of Canarsie that had some type of plant growth that were about 10 feet tall, and it had a path between them that you could run your horse. And I recall the sister of Jim Wheadon yelling to me because she was on the ground and the horse was in the thickets. Romance-wise I did take the sister to the movies one night, and her brother came along with her, so I believe that basically I could have gone with the brother and had the sister come along.

Congratulations to me, I came across a note that on November the 8th of the year 2002, I celebrated my golden wedding anniversary. And I believe the secret of lasting that long is to be "temporarily" separated for 40 years. In the art field, I was very much impressed with Norman Rockwell, who did covers for the Saturday Evening Post, a now defunct magazine but very popular at one time. I sent him an idea for a cover, explaining that there should be a contrast between some old houses and new television aerials on the roof. He sent me back a letter with a drawing of a dog with his signature, and thanked me, and he put that idea on the cover of the Post which was interesting to have this broken down type of house with two men on the roof trying to install the television antenna.

Why I ran from the bullies for the most part, if I wish to be honest with myself, I believe I did not want to get hurt physically. However when I was in my early 20's I decided to prove to myself that it was not really fright, it was goodness that was in me, so I entered the New York Daily news Golden Gloves. It was one purpose of the newspaper to help those who wish to get started in pugilism too, to have some base where they could learn the excitement of the "fight game". I put in anywhere I was required to go for a physical examination and eventually got involved with fighting somebody that the newspapers representatives believed was about equal to my strengths.

All I had to supply were my own boxing shoes, my own athletic supporter, and my own mouthpiece (and my own blood). I do believe that the business of professional fighting is like any other business, but in the fight business, the blood shows. Looking back on it from this time frame, I would say it was rather gutsy of me to have put that part of the fight adventure into my life. I could have gotten seriously hurt. I got to the arena 2 hours before the first fight was to begin. I never went for the scheduled physical exam because it was interfering with what was my social schedule for that original date. He found my blood pressure to be a bit high and said I could not fight and I said "Very good, I'm going home" (relieved that this burden was taken off me without my own consent). However the doctor said "Well rest a bit, we'll see what happens", so I sat there, and 20 minutes later, the doctor came over to me and my pressure was normal enough for me to be in the "fight racket". Actually I knew nothing about boxing because I never had a pair of boxing gloves on in my entire life. What I did was I bought a book entitled "How to Box".

Chapter 9

Time for comedy relief: These two Irishmen are sitting on a plane that's flying to Ireland, and the Captain comes in and says, "We have a problem with one engine. It isn't working, but we have three engines and the plane should arrive safely. It'll just take us a bit longer." He comes back a bit later, the Captain does, and says: "Another engine has stopped on us, but we still have two engines and this plane is equipped to fly safely with the two engines. We'll arrive but it will take us a little bit longer than we thought before the first engine quit." Later on, the Captain comes in and he announces that the third engine is no longer working, but the plane is so well built that it can still reach the destination safely. However, it's going to take considerably longer than originally scheduled. So one Irishmen turns to the other and says, "If the last engine stops on us, we'll be up here all night!."

The secretary story goes on as follows; eventually I would take Sally to a motel in New Jersey, and I would have beer and wine. We would watch television. Eventually wind up in bed, but fully clothed, and a bit of love making would commence. I would fall asleep and so would Sally. We would awake at about five in the morning, and I would have to drive her back home in Brooklyn, which is quite a drive across the Washington Bridge and down the highway to her house, and then return all the way back up the same route to my place in Pearl River, New York, which is also a considerable trip. I would arrive at my house just in time to take my daughter for her piano lesson at nine. I don't know what story Sally would give to her husband for her arriving in the house at seven on a Saturday morning, after being out all night long, but I was able to convince my wife that I would be sleeping at the downtown athletic club after a night of entertainment at the facility. I believe she wanted to acknowledge that as the truth because this had been happening every Friday night for about a year.

Of course, my artwork was getting to be less of an importance to me whereby I was having my art teacher do most of the work for me on portraits that I had scheduled clients, and would do a little bit of touch up work myself so I felt honest. I would tell the person when they paid me the money that I did have some help from my art teacher, but I never told them that it was about 99% of the work that she was doing. Though I wanted to stay with my faith, I didn't go much more beyond the "by-the-book" standards of Catholicism. I did go to mass every Sunday and Holy Day, but didn't got to confession or receive communion because I was not ready to give up Sally, and that way of life I had chosen to live. In fact, Sunday was a joke, I would go to mass early because I would get up about an hour earlier than necessary so I could get myself drunk on wine and go to mass by myself and return to take my wife and children to a later mass. Although I had attended mass bodily, I don't know how much I was being true to my faith because I was dead drunk when I attended the holy sacrifice of the mass. I used the excuse of going to an earlier mass by myself because I was going to prepare the Sunday dinner and thereby I knew when I got back from the services, I could continue to drink as I was preparing the meal. By the time the meal was prepared and it was rather fanciful because they had the best foods available for myself and the family including shrimp cocktail, lobster tails, and pate de fois gras, and truffles, etc., at the time when I should enjoying the meal with the family, I was ready to pass out because I had at least two quarts Muscatel wine in me by that time on a Sunday afternoon.

Monday morning was always an experience where I would listen to the men tease me about having a secretary that didn't talk to me and in my mind knowing that I was with her on Friday night, and you people who are giving me a hard times now about this situation would have loved to have been with her yourselves. Ironically, everyone in the organization I worked for believed that I was the ideal "church going" family man dedication to the organization's welfare. At this in my memoir, I believe that things were working to go against me as far as my career, my family, and my faith. December was party time in my business, at least one or two invitations per day, luncheons and dinners. I had been out late on Monday, Tuesday, and Wednesday around the Christmas holiday time and I could hardly wait to go to my bed on Thursday. Sally insisted on seeing me Thursday night and I made arrangements somehow to stay away from the house on Thursday. Sally said she would meet me near the restaurant where she would be dining with one of the other married men in the office. I waited in my car from six to eight in the evening, drinking at the same time, sitting in the car and I waited in the car until nine and then came ten, and Sally didn't arrive so I decided to drive home. I had gotten within one mile of my house in the winding country-type roads they had in Rockland County and I fell asleep at the wheel of my car. I ran into an unoccupied parked car on the road, crushing my car and putting my head through the windshield of my car, causing me to go into shock. As I put my hand to my forehead I felt my skull bone so it must have been quite a tear in the flesh covering the skull. The people in the house came running out when they heard the noise and must've seen how bad a condition I was in, so they called for an ambulance and asked me to come in their house and sit down. My beautiful new car was a complete wreck and so was I, because I told the people "I'll be okay I believe I could walk home." Meanwhile the people had put a towel around my forehead to staunch the flow of whatever blood might be coming from my head.

Awaiting the ambulance because I was definitely a surgery case. I was taken to Nyack Hospital located in Nyack, New York, where a neurosurgeon happened to be on duty although this was about midnight. At that time I wasn't sure whether I would live or not considering the seriousness of the situation. So, I asked for a Catholic priest for the last rites because I wanted to "square myself with the Almighty." As I was lying on the table, I heard the surgeon talking to my priest from my hometown in Pearl River and as far as I know the conversation was something to the effect that I should be alright and I would be able to have visitors in the morning, at that moment everything went blank. The next morning when I awoke in the hospital bed, the neurosurgeon said "You'll be alright except you might have some pains in the chest because that's where I started pounding your heart when it had stopped!" It's interesting on checking back on this that I recall saying to the surgeon that I have to go to work tomorrow, and the surgeon trying to placate me, said "Well, maybe the day after, but at the moment rest." There was a hairline fracture of the skull, and stitches from one side of my forehead to the other so I believe I would be fortunate to even walk out of the hospital within a month, not a day. I was contacted by the towing company who collected the car or what was left of it and they offered me $75 for the car as junk which I was eager to accept. I was more eager to have the towing fellow to remove all the bottles which were empty and half empty, and any possible evidence of my connections with Sally. According to my firm, I was still Mr. Nice Guy and received from my business contacts flowers and condolences and everything necessary for me to try to cheer up and get out of the hospital and come back to be a party man again.

Sally phoned me at the hospital and said she was going to come up to Nyack, New York, and visit me which was a bit of a problem because my wife was visiting me. Some of the scenes were something out of a Marx brother movie and I tried to keep my wife and Sally separated whereby one was coming in one door and the other was going out the other door and I got away with it for the entire hospital stay. I wonder how Sally was able to get away from her husband for all the time she was visiting me and even more so for all the nights we had been together where she was coming in, as noted, before five or six in the morning. One of the bigger mistakes was me going along with Sally's request that I meet her before I go back to work officially. The following was going to be something out of a detective novel how I was able to have somebody in town call me on the phone, and me answer and pretend that it was the company who insisted that I get back to work on the Friday before the Monday that I was to officially start work. I arranged for someone in town to call my house and when I answered they were to hang up and I gave the story out loud that I would be hesitant in returning to work before I was supposed to, of course so my wife could hear this. Unbeknown to me, Sally had set a trap for me because she was tired of waiting for me to divorce my wife and marry her. Sally had left one of the cards that I gave her that had sentiments of love attached to it and it was for her husband to see the morning that we got together for that Friday tryst.

I had been in the motel with Sally for the day drinking, eating, and general carousing and time had gone by for me to get back to my house. I phoned my wife to say that I was on my way home and she told me over the phone that she knows the whole story of Sally and me because all hell had broke loose. Sally's husband found the card and my wife Irene had phoned the office because she was upset as to why I had to get back to work on that Friday. In all of the eighteen years I had worked there, never once had my wife called for any reason. I went into a kind of shock at that point because my wife said she knew of what was going on in my life and "You just wait until you get home." I had several thousand dollars on me when I left for work and not too sure of what happened for the next two months because I was spending the money on drinks and food with Sally as though there wasn't an end to the supply. Eventually the money was gone and I decided to take Sally back to her husband and I was going back to my wife, but there was something more than our returns to our spouses which made the rest of our adventures serious. Apparently, Sally's husband took her back and my wife accepted me, although two months had passed since me and Sally went carousing. My wife said I could sleep in the spare bedroom until I found other accommodations. The company released me with no recommendations and no severance pay due to the scandal caused by my and Sally's behavior. I was also blackballed in the area of expertise that I was in so I could not get work for which I had experience and education, the eighteen years of devoted service meaning nothing to the directors. My wife went to the marriage court and got a legal separation whereby the judge gave her the five children, the bank books and the estate; and ordering me to pay my wife a certain amount of money every month. To me this was a bit of a joke because I was basically unemployed trying to understand how I was going to keep that lifestyle without the type of position that gave me the money to live in that manner. I purchased a second hand used car jalopy with some of the money that were available to me from a company pension fund and whatever mistake it was from there on, came when I called Sally to find out how she was getting along. She asked me to meet with her again and we wound up on the road, the two of us now living very desperately in a situation that had no glamour to it in the very least. Sally's husband had divorced her, naming me as the other party and she was free enough for living that type of life in a car with me. Meanwhile, this Texan and Alaskan are talking and the Alaskan says to the Texan, "If you don't stop bragging about how big Texas is I'll see to it that they cut Alaska in half and make Texas the third biggest state." As for Sally and I, it is strange to think that an attractive lady like her was willing to spend time with me in a junk car, no longer the fancy motel rooms and the fancy dining. I at least was able to panhandle enough for wine and get by my day staying in a stupor.

I was able to shave in the bathrooms of gasoline stations and that was about as close to personal hygiene as I was able to get, no showers or bathing facilities available. Oddly enough, I didn't think alcohol was the root of the problem at the time, still trying to get myself in order some day so I'd be able to get back to that type of lifestyle I once knew. As many times as I tried to smoke cigarettes in my life, I was never able to get used to it, although Sally was a smoker. It added to my problem because I not only had to panhandle for any drinking money, I had to get enough money together for Sally's cigarettes. We had gotten with "the kindness of strangers," i.e. my going into a diner and asking for a sandwich. Since I believed that this was only a temporary setback in my life, I would put down the address of the gas station and the name of the station for all those that were giving me gas on my story about being up against it and could they help me out. I just had to be careful about not using the same station twice, although I still had it in my mind that I was going to repay these kind people. This included the restaurants that had given us food, one in particular being Mary's Diner. I went in with Sally and asked if they could possibly be able to help the both of us out with a sandwich and such because we were down on our luck and quite hungry at the time. The owner, Mary, said that if we wanted to we could eat there three times a day, her providing the breakfast, lunch, and dinner at no charge to either of us. What a kind lady, and I used my philosophy in this case which states, "Shoot for the moon, if you miss you will still be among the stars."

Since this book covers a period of time where I have to go back in memory over forty years, the time sequence may be a specialty of this book. At one point Sally and I were in the car for two days without me moving it because there was a dead battery and I had no money to get it recharged. Eventually I took the battery to a garage and gave them a story and they recharged my battery expecting money sometime in the future. This was in a fairly upscale town in New Jersey outside of Bergen Park and the residents may have reported us to the police as potential troublemakers. This scene you have to picture, me walking down towards my car with the recharged battery in a box, ready to install it and be on our way. The small town police must have thought that I was John Dillinger because there were motorcycle police, squad car police, every side road blocked off with police cars waiting for my arrival. Sally was still so attractive and charming that she had given the police such a story that they felt so sorry for us and even offered to install the battery, which they did and we drove away from that town. One more thing to add to this soap opera is that Sally's brother is a police officer and he was looking for us in the New Jersey area and apparently he had been at one of those gas stations with our ID photos trying to find out any information about his sister. As I found out later he was going to put a bullet in my head and resign from the force, turning in his badge and gun not caring what was going to happen to him. As it so happened, I returned to one of the gas stations where I had previously gotten gas on trust and the owner told me to wait for a minute while he went to get something from inside his office. Before I knew it there I was with the Fort Lee New Jersey police department asking us to accompany them to the police station, figuring that we were some type of criminals because of the owner in the station believed we were wanted criminals because of a search by a New York City police officer. After detaining us at the station house for a good part of the day, the desk sergeant said to Sally and I the following remark which still is a bit of a hurt, "You can go now. The FBI doesn't want you, the state, city, and county police don't want you, your wife and husband don't want either one of you, and we don't want you, so get out!"

I took Sally back to her Brooklyn home and I went back to my place in Pearl River New York hoping that there might be another chance somehow. Sally of course now is living with her mother having been divorced, and my wife still willing to give me another chance despite all of the happenings. I was able to get work at the Dugan Brother's bakery as a raw material buyer. I had been working there several weeks when I made the mistake of calling Sally to find out how she was getting along. She said we should meet and I did on a weeknight, where we stayed at a motel again and the next day I called the office to let them know that I will be coming in later. The secretary said that there was somebody there waiting for me which I relayed to Sally and she became somewhat upset and before you knew it, there we were on the road again. Sally and I with all our affects attached to living in an automobile. Previous to this I had gotten a job at the Journal News in West Nyack, New York and I worked there in the morning from 5 am to 11 am taking care of the AP and UPI machines, my duties primarily consisted of giving ticker tapes to the editors. I was told how to know when a story ended by the feeling of the ticker tape having a number thirty on it, and I would put these tapes on wall nailed together with the story that would come out of the machine for the editor. It was amazing how much I needed to drink that I would go out to my parked car outside the building and get myself several gulps of wine, run back in and try to keep up with the tapes that were starting to pile up on the floor. Once when I had gotten a bit behind because of the drinking I gathered all that was lying on the floor and threw them into the wastebasket figuring all of it didn't really matter anyway. I found out what I had done is throw away a continuing story from the UPI machine. There again Sally wanted me to meet her and I would get into my car and drive all the way from West Nyack, New York to Flatbush, Brooklyn, be with her for about an hour or so and then travel all the way back to Pearl River in time for my wife to not be totally suspicious of my whereabouts because she had taken me back.

Concerning the last episode with Sally, Mary at the diner had gotten me a job working for a landscaper. In my interview with the owner of the business he said to me that some of his men made as much as $300 a week. I found out later when I was out there sweating with some of the men, they said that once we made that in the spring we worked seven days a week, we worked from six in the morning until midnight. It was a dirty job, sweaty, hot, and backbreaking. I recall part of it was getting rid of the junk grass and weeds and everything else that we put into the truck. These were taken to the Jersey dumps and I do especially find it vivid in my mind that here I am in the middle of the New Jersey dumps with a one-hundred degree temperature and I'm unloading garbage. I recall Sally and I on the 4th of July sitting at the side of the road with no gas for the car, no cigarettes, no wine, no money for food, and the temperature well above 100 degrees. Somehow I was able to get Sally back to her mother and me back to my Pearl River home with not exactly open arms from my wife, but acceptance. I had now gotten a job working in a carwash in Spring Valley, New York where my mother was living in one of the resort cabins I had gotten for her. Sally had the address of the cabin and one day I found in the mail a postcard with nothing on it but a drawing of a telephone and a tear drop coming from the receiver. I called her and found out she was now eight months pregnant with my soon-to-be-born child.

Chapter 10

Talk about continuity, I hope my last tape was about me and the Golden Gloves. If not there I was in the dressing room looking for all these people wondering which one was going to be the one who I'm going to get knocked out by. I was by myself and the others all had handlers and at the time for protecting your hands, tape was given out by the newspaper representatives. I was given three strips of tape for each hand to put on by myself, and the others were given tapes that looked like they had plaster of Paris on their hands. That's how much tape they had. Eventually, I was told to go down to the boxing ring and sit by the corner where I was to be the fighter for the next fight. I'm sitting there with my overcoat and some fellow comes over to me and says "If you're any good I'm going to take you into my stable of fighters, and we'll move you along until you're the champ." I'm thinking to myself I just hope you don't have to help the referee carry my carcass out of the ring. Just a side thought, why do they call it a boxing ring, when it's obviously square?

The bell sounds and I go out to the middle of the ring and I take up the boxing stance as was in the book that I purchased, entitled "How to box" and boom, I'm knocked across the ring and I'm laying on my back. There is a mandatory eight count when I get up from the floor. I return to the middle of the ring where I take up the same boxing stance and boom, boom, another couple of punches and I'm laying down somewhere on the other side of the ring again with a mandatory eight count when I get to my feet. I proceed to the middle of the ring again, but the referee stops the fight. Apparently, there's a ruling in the Golden Gloves that if you're down twice in the same round your opponent wins the bout. They took me back to the dressing room where I got the gloves off, the tape off, but I did get a Golden Gloves lapel pin, which I cherished through the years. However, there was a photo of me in the newspaper the next day, as I was half way down with the description that I recall to this day "Dave Mahoney of West Hemstead, follows through after lashing out at Vince Seplesky of Levittown." Officially that was the end of my in-ring career, one of the shortest in history. Spiritual thought: Lord, teach me to want what I already have.

This is the story of Sally. As I was trying to keep my two lives separated as best as I was able to, the organization gave me a new secretary, who was a beauty, very efficient, and was very much desired by all of the men in the department, if not in the entire building. Sally was married to a very handsome Irishman and I was trying to concentrate on my work, but I found that she was getting to be a problem. I tried desperately to keep her at a distance from my feelings, to a point where there was no conversation between us other than the basic necessities of getting the work finished. I appreciated her efficiency, so much that whenever I happened to be out at any gathering and I wasn't coming back to the office, I could let her handle whatever needed to be done with a belief that there would be no problem with her executing the balance of the workload. It was at one of the holiday parties that I offered to give Sally a lift to her house with my car and our relationship began at that time, it was an affair, but I still kept to my motto of sex being apart of marriage. Sally and I went partying at least once a week for the next week without anyone in the office, or my wife having any idea of those said arrangements with myself and Sally. Since I wasn't outwardly pursuing Sally as the other men were, they believed that there was a problem between the two of us. There again, I took Sally to all the places I could readily be seen by my colleagues in the same business field. A thought: I used to dine with President Harry Truman after he was no longer the President of the United States, and I recall one anecdote—he claimed that when he went back to Independence, Missouri from the White House the reporters meaning well, asked him what he was going to do, either write a book or go on a lecturing tour. Harry replied "The first thing I'm going to do is take my luggage upstairs and put my clothes away."

I thought about a lady I know who is somewhat disturbing as far as her dealing with other people is concerned, she isn't that well liked by others of her nature. I tried to help as much as I could on a monthly basis. We would go to lunch together in Manhattan. One day at lunch she told me about the special, it involved chicken, cheese sticks, and several other little items for about six dollars and that day we had the special. When she returned I was chewing on the cheese sticks and making light conversation with her and had a small coffee, and a small piece of cake and I gave her the six dollars. When I got home I thought to myself that is rather a steep price for some cheese sticks, a piece of cake and coffee. Therefore, I phoned her and asked her what made the price six dollars for several small items, and in her own ditzy way she said "Oh that's right, they gave us chicken also but I left it at the counter instead of brining it to the table, silly me." Also sillier me because I didn't think to ask at the time as to what the balance of the meal would be.

Back to Sally, she said she had an unhappy marriage and I replied that I had a very bad marriage as well. In fact, I went so far as to let Sally know that I was going to divorce my wife and marry her. It never occurred to me that there was the possibility that Sally wouldn't be able to get a divorce. That is an example of why I was drinking more than I should have been because the alcohol was dulling my senses. It's interesting to me that this day I have an attitude as far as my relationship with Sally was concerned, is that since there wasn't any penetration I was still within my idea of not having sex outside of my marriage. Do you realize that race car spelt backwards is still race car; and the only person to win both the Nobel Prize and an academy award was George Bernard Shaw. He obtained one Nobel Prize for his writing and he received an Oscar for the screenplay to Pygmalion that he wrote. I should talk about my airplanes I had in Pearl River, New York. It's also a way of lying without telling the truth, if I told people that I used to fly airplanes at a local field near my home, it would be the truth. However, they were model planes that I was interested in. I built free flights, gasoline engine powered and I had gotten to the point of a radio controlled biplane, which I never had the courage to take off the ground for fear of it crashing. I was able to get the other men in the carpool interested in this hobby, and they had quite a time of it at the airfield on Sunday afternoons. Me being a little bit upset when one of them who had spent two months building a free flight stood there and watched it disappear because of the gasoline engine taking it too far into the sky to catch current, which took it out of sight. I had one of mine disappear because I hadn't set the gas engine to the correct amount of gas and it disappeared into the woods.

My son and one of the neighbor children went with me into the woods and searched until dark and I got an interesting reply from the neighbor's boy as we gave up for the day looking for the plane. He said "Oh well, back to the drawing board." "Back to the drawing board, this plane took me three months to construct and now it's gone!" One other plane that had gotten into the woods I was able to locate, but it was at the top of a tree and I had to use an axe to get the tree down before I could get my plane back to my house. I would have my name and address on a sticker on the body of the plane in case they did get lost, and it was fortunate that one of the lost planes was returned to me by some fellow on a Saturday afternoon, who came to my house and was able to locate me by the return sticker.

Chapter 11

Well anyway I gave notice to the National Distiller's people and in about a week's time, I was over at the Near East College Association, which did the purchasing of all the supplies for 13 universities and hospitals, which was quite a demanding position because you certainly had to know a little about all types of products for those institutions. As I've learned, the alcoholic has a personality to be become a workaholic when they're in sobriety, and I certainly was the workaholic; taking folders and files home on the weekends, working ten, twelve hours a day. This was noticed by the powers to be, eventually I was given a higher position in the company and eventually became in charge of the entire department which was a better position in power and finances than I ever had in my other careers. In fact, I was able to send my wife three times the amount of money the courts decided she should get each month. Well I now had a private office decorated in wall to wall money, a private secretary, and the respect that I once had in the business world. Everything was going well now as far as my career and my dealings with Sally and my status quo with the family in Pearl River, New York. My children were growing up without me and the child I had with Sally was almost a reminder of my attention being paid to this infant instead of where my marriage vows had directed me, my conscience was subconsciously getting me as far as this living condition was concerned. I was still dealing with Sally's alcoholic mother and trying to keep some semblance of sanity in these conditions while I was desperately trying to hold onto a very responsible, well paying position in Manhattan. An interesting thought: Egyptian men wore eye makeup, apparently there was a problem with flies at the time that might irritate the eye and cause blindness, and the makeup would keep the flies away from the eyes.

Back to my life where things would get so bad at the house that I would leave and wind up somewhere in Manhattan, trying to make it on my own. Sally would phone me at the office and let me know that her mother was going to be different and things were going to be at peace in the household, and I would return, only to find that nothing had changed. This type of occurrence happened several times, and I decided that something was very wrong, my living this type of life and still trying to be at peace with my higher power that I call God. I would go to mass daily, during my noontime lunch hour, and I would go to mass on the weekends when Sally thought I would be at an AA meeting. I was actually going to an evening mass, trying to stay at one with God. Of course I couldn't receive the sacraments because I wasn't fully ready to change this way of life I was living, although I desperately wanted conditions to be more to my own liking and to what I believed the higher power wanted for me.

I made a big decision with the grace of God, deciding to get another apartment of my own somewhere. I was able to find a furnished apartment and pay the rent for the month and then told Sally that I was leaving. To say the least there was a lot of commotion because nobody suspected I was truly leaving for good this time because they know I had come back several times previously. To jump way ahead of this book, I was just reminded of an experience where I am living currently in Borough Park, Brooklyn. I was to meet a friend of mine at a train station in Queens and he was going to take me to lunch, a Wall Street fellow that I had gotten a very good position for through my contacts, the appointed time was about 11 am. When I got downstairs to get to the subway, and by the way my friend had no cell phone or any other way to contact him, he was going to be on the subway platform, and I found out that there was cement work being done on the sidewalk, in front of my house, making it impossible for me to go through the front of the building. The house owner told me I couldn't go through the front because of the cemented sidewalk, but he thought if you came through his apartment on the ground floor, you could go through the back and then through someone's front yard, and in turn, be on your merry way. When I entered the backyard of the house owner, he said "You'll have to climb over this chain link fence, which was about seven feet tall, and had a three foot wall bottom at the bottom of the fence." Add to this the rain that was pouring down and also I had an umbrella and a cane and the owner says well if you can't climb over, there's a hole in the fence at the far end you can climb through that hole. You'll have to picture this, but there I was, trying to get through this two foot square hole in the fence with my umbrella and cane, and one foot over the cement wall on the bottom through the fence, and my shoulders, back, and head all contorted, trying to get through the barbed edges of the broken cyclone fence. Another anecdote about the same living space concerns my trying to open the door to my apartment on the third floor of the building and having a problem with the key opening the lock I stepped back and I wound up going backwards down all fifteen steps, hitting my head against the plaster wall pushing my head through the wall and my back, neck, and head—all bruised, whereby I now put a small picture over the hole in the wall which I refer to as my memorial head bash.

Dear reader, please consider your efforts to tolerate the poor writing, grammar, and punctuation as your opportunity to practice tolerance, thank you. Maybe a bit of time to lighten up a bit on this memoir of mine. Moses is talking to God and says, "I can't understand you giving all this rich oil land to our enemies and you want us to cut off the tip of our what?!" By the way, you might also excuse my poor spelling. I'm not sure what direction I'm headed in at the moment in the book because of time frames, lapses, memories, etc. However, the point comes where I was diagnosed with a brain tumor, which had grown to the size of a grapefruit. I went through a ten hour operation to remove the tumor, and stayed at the hospital for four months to aid in the healing with physical and occupational therapy. Apparently the tumor had destroyed an optic nerve in the brain which controls the vision, and I had gone blind technically, basically with only vague outlines from only one eye, whereas the other eye had no sight at all. I somehow went back to Sally and was trying to make my life somewhat tolerable without any type of aftercare rehabilitation, still trying to maintain my sobriety. Since I was told in my AA experience, there's no reason to drink, only excuses; I'm now believing I had a reason, poor eyesight. At that time the only things that I was holding onto was my faith and God, and my decision to put off the drink of alcohol for one more day. Always hoping that something would develop which would restore my sight and give me back normalcy in my career.

I went to all the best ophthalmologists in the state of New York and each one gave me their opinion after all the testing that there was nothing they could do for my vision, me still hoping against hope and wound up with one ophthalmologist who said to me, "Vincent, you must face the fact that this is your way of life now, limited vision, so I'd suggest you do something about putting your life in order under these conditions." At about this time I went to the New York State Commission for the blind and asked them for their assistance in reshaping my life. They presented me with a cane and enrolled me in the training program of the Industrial Home for the Blind, located in New Hyde Park, Long Island, New York. I was living in Brighton Beach and that meant that I had to be up at about 5 am and travel by subway to the bus in downtown Brooklyn, which would take me out to New Hyde Park, approximately forty miles from the city and leave me at the school for training.

In the evening I would return to the starting point, by taking the bus and the train back to my Brighton Beach apartment. This was a tiresome and draining experience, but I stayed with it until I changed to another rehabilitation center in the city of Manhattan, where I'd be getting instruction at the Jewish Guild for the Blind. Their bus would pick me up at my apartment in Flatbush, which I'm a little bit out of touch as to how I wound up at that apartment, but I'll explain as I clear up. They would take me to mid-Manhattan every day and from 10 am to 4 pm, I learned all the techniques about making mops and brooms (which I hated to do with a passion.) It involved sitting at a table for about six hours and putting together a type of erector set, electrical equipment, or some wood working equipment; this was meant to improve hand-mind coordination. What I found irritating was the people who would come through the area where we were working on these projects, whereby these tours of benefactors to the school could gawk at us as if we were all some type of zoo animals.

My experience is tapping around with a cane, which is called mobility, I found a challenge which you may have heard of from the film "Around the World in 80 Days," consider my experiences around the block in 80 days. Oddly enough, my mobility instructor had a drinking problem and he was trying to give me safety instructions on how to get by with a cane as my help for navigation. Although I regret it now, but not that much because of the availability of the electronics industry, I decided to learn Braille. That was basically to get me out of that repetitive hand-mind coordination technique that was getting to be annoying after five or six hours straight, knowing that at least I'll have one hour learning in the Braille classroom. In some sense that was a mistake because previously to this I could go home and that was it until the next day with no real concerns except the travel to the school and back home again, whereas with the Braille, I had to study after I left the classes. This meant on the way home on the train I was studying my Braille and I studied it during my lunch hours, and before and after AA meetings—sometimes during an AA meeting. As I progressed in the Braille studies, I was advanced to a type of shorthand Braille whereby a few little dots could be a whole sentence, however it enabled me to read the New York Times.

I don't think a lot of people know that the New York Times puts out an edition for the blind, which is interesting because without the advertising and so on, the thickness of the paper in it's entirety is about the same as it would be in print. I might say this that anyone who's read the New York Times in print will find what I went through trying to read that newspaper with raised dots. Actually, there were times when I was so frustrated with the Braille when all the dots began to feel the same to me that I wanted to throw the Braille work out the window and jump out after it. An interesting fact on Braille is that Louis Braille in France, who was blind since the age of three put together the Braille system named after him and the French Government wouldn't approve of it because they had too much money invested in the embossed method type of instruction for the blind in that country. Also, Louis Braille was one of the best organists in Europe at the age of 12 years old and was picked on by the children in the school because of his proficiency in music and I can tell you that the blind can be cruel to one another because there's a type of vision which is referred to as legally blind, where you could only make out vague outlines (my case.) They would trip Louis Braille any time they had the chance by putting their canes in front of him and generally made life miserable for him in blind children's school; so much so that he ran away one day and as he was out in the streets in France, he became a little bit disconnected as to what was happening since he had no sight and thought possibly a horse and carriage may run him over. I recall his quote, “Well if that happens, so much the better.”

I have had that thought go through my mind when I’m a little bit upset with street crossings, etc. That’s not what life is about, we keep on going. Well, back to the blind school, I found that many of the students were either thinking about drinking, talking about drinking, talking about their hangovers, and also discussing as to where they were going to meet after school to do some more drinking. I was able to conclude that many of them were alcoholics who were in dyer need of treatment. What I did was speak to the psychologist in the school and she told me that they couldn’t do anything with the drinkers in the school, all they do is terminate them from their studies. Then they’d be in more trouble because they’ve got a drinking problem and don’t become responsible human beings in society. At about this time I must have had about ten years sobriety in AA and I would speak to the students one on one and try to get them to go to AA meetings and basically pull themselves together at least until they got through the school training. The instructors’ time the students as opposed to the sighted in the area of making mops and brooms and I eventually became one of the fastest people in the school, and quite the proficient mop and broom maker.

Despite my qualifications I learned that there wasn’t any room for more employees in the mop and broom factory, so having an interesting example of working with the higher power and having things done in the Almighty’s good time. As much as I hated making mops and brooms I thought it would at least keep me occupied during the day and will also possibly help me get to another step for whatever is available in the blind occupation area. I was asking my higher power to please get me an opening in that mop and broom factory and I’d certainly do my best there even though I despised the labor involved. Eventually, after six months of waiting I decided to change my direction, thinking that maybe the world had enough mops and brooms and possibly use a person in the field of alcoholism. I decided to go into the field and get the education needed to become helpful in the field. I don’t know if I could do it again, but I enrolled in Rutgers School of Alcohol Studies in New Brunswick, New Jersey. I stayed in a campus dormitory, sometimes I think that they should’ve given me the diploma just for finding the buildings because they were located all over the town of New Brunswick and that meant street crossings, and squares, circles, up and down steps, all of which was quite the challenge. Then finding the classroom inside the building, then knowing the work. They weren’t that easy on people who couldn’t keep up with the others whereby they kept it as serious business that if weren’t able to keep up, go make mops and brooms. Interesting when I check back on the business of no opportunity and the factory and making an opportunity at the college for myself that God wanted me in another field, not mops and brooms but where the unfortunate could get help from a person who had the "book learning" about alcoholics. Actually, Rutgers University is one of the few national research centers on alcoholism in the United States for the government and they cannot come up with the reason causing people to drink. It doesn't make sense why one person will drink or become an alcoholic and another person, even in the same family, will not become an alcoholic with the same amount of drink, which leads to what they call theories on the disease of alcoholism. I might add that the American Medical Association has declared alcoholism as an incurable disease with treatable symptoms.

An interesting anecdote on the graduation dinner which was held prior to graduation in the school cafeteria; they had before dinner speakers, not after dinner speakers, and one fellow speaking was Vernon Johnson who'd written a book on alcoholism entitled "I'll Quit Tomorrow." Naturally all the students including myself were anxious to get to the food because we had enough of the alcoholism concerns during the school study times and training times. Vernon kept on talking and talking and talking, and apparently a note was put in my hand by my roommate and he said pass this note along and whispered to me that the note reads as follows; which is a take off on Johnson's book "I'll quit tomorrow." It stated "He'll quit tomorrow." I recall interestingly enough that when the time came for the president of the school to give his talk, he said the following and it sounded like something from Shakespeare, "Welcome to the field counseling, you now have the privilege of helping alcoholics and their families! From this day on, if you want love and affection, go out and get yourself a dog!" I returned from Rutgers to my Brooklyn apartment and made attempts to get into the field of alcoholism treatment. There was this General they called "Spit and Polish." That's because he was always spitting as he was Polish.

To get ahead of the game there was a fellow named Jerry who had a motorcycle about ten feet long, a tremendously big, almost like a car type of driving machine, and Jerry was looking for a place to live. I knew somebody from the McAllister tugboat family and I would visit this lady on a regular basis and she said he could come live with her in her apartment, she had an extra room. I told Jerry to come over, and he came with his motorcycle and left it in the street. Angie McAllister told him when he came up that he couldn't leave his motorcycle in the street, it'd be stolen. Jerry went downstairs and got the motorcycle into the lobby of this fancy building, got it into the small elevator somehow, and got it up to the 6th floor where Angie lived, and got it out of the elevator, down the hall into her apartment. Well, Jerry had a place to stay, as did his bike.

I recall when Sandy and her husband, Tony, who owned this corporation, invited my wife and me out to the racetrack one night. After we came back from the racetrack, we stopped in at Lundy's in Sheepshead Bay, Brooklyn, a very famous seafood house. We ordered drinks and appetizers which were served, as for the balance of the meal, the waiter said we wouldn't be served because the kitchen was closed and Sandy got very upset. She offered to pay for what little we had, but only to Mr. Lundy, she wasn't trying to get out of paying it she implied, but she wanted to inform Mr. Lundy of the circumstances of the evening as to why weren't served the balance of our meal. The maitre d came over to us and apologized for the mix up and declared the drinks and appetizers as being on them, there wasn't any charge, whereas Sandy obliged and thanked them and placed a ten-dollar bill on the table for the waiter's tip, this was to show that she wasn't cheap and we were within our rights to a full meal.

Chapter 12

I might say a word about the pregnancy of Sally, we eventually had normal sex and I must say I was almost an animal about it. In fact, Sally mentioned to me that we had at least eighty-nine orgasms in eleven days. I might share an interesting thought on the pregnancy; I had gotten a little tearful one time and I told Sally that my father was a naval hero and there hasn't been anyone named after him and I believed in retrospect, that we should have a child and name him after my father. I now believe it was the alcohol in me that was talking like that because I had no idea that the child would indeed be a male, but Sally agreed and this was now the result. Meanwhile, I had gotten a fairly good position with the Maritime Overseas Corporation in Manhattan which required me to be there from 9 to 5, Monday through Friday. My diligence in landscaping the car wash surrounding area paid off in one sense because to help me get this Maritime Overseas position, I had stated that I was the manager of a string of service stations on the east coast and the owner of the carwash backed me up as a reference. I may have mentioned previously in this tape that I worked for Bohacks as a garbage room cleaner, stocking shelves, and eventually a cashier. I was efficient although I was drinking through all of those areas of work, but I was a very devoted supermarket man and that was noticed by the manager.

I recall one day when I was reported by two customers at 10 in the morning that I'd been drinking, the manager had asked me to go home for the day and return the next day, that was on a Thursday. The next thing that I remember is that I was in a cheap hotel room on a Monday morning wondering what the heck happened with Friday and Saturday. I phoned the fellow at Bohacks and he told me if I were to report to work on Tuesday morning sober I'd still have my job. Later on I used this fellow as a reference that I was the buyer for Bohack's East Coast district for all of their canned goods and I had used the store address as the main buying office. I'm now back living in the house with my wife and children and things seem to be going along well. However, I had gone to the doctor with a cough and he said to me that I should go to the hospital immediately because I had pneumonia. I told the doctor that three of my children were in the hospital as of now at that time and I wasn't going to go into the hospital myself, so he told me if I didn't go I would have a problem, but he gave me a list of items I'd be able to get over the counter so I might get through it. I took the bus from Pearl River to the Manhattan Transit Authority building on 42nd Street which is a considerable ride, and once I got there I had to take a bus across town to 5th Avenue to get my place of employment, all of this with active pneumonia. A side thought on that incident, is that I was now a smoker and when I was at the drug store, as I was getting the list of everything the doctor gave me, I said throw in a pack of cigarettes. I smoked through that pneumonia even though each time I took a puff it was like a knife sticking me in my chest because of the cough that followed shortly after.

Because of the weakness caused by the pneumonia and other circumstances, I wasn't doing the job as well as I should have been; hearing the directors talking about me one day that they'd probably have to release me. Meanwhile, I had told my wife that instead of me commuting from Pearl River everyday, which was a good two hours, I was going to take up residence in a hotel in Manhattan near the job so I could be at work within five minutes time and back to my resting place in about five minutes time also. I might add that I hadn't been drinking for approximately one month's time since I got the new position and had it in my mind that when I got to that hotel I was going to start drinking. This day that I went there with all my clothing and put my car in a garage near the hotel, I purchased a bottle of Muscatel wine and went to the hotel room and proceeded to drink. Actually, at that time the organization had terminated me but they gave me an interesting out on the "firing", as they said I could come into work everyday and they'll pay me, but if I ever get an outside job interview to take off and go for the possible other work place which I thought was very generous of the firm. It's amazing what active alcoholism can do the one's mind because I called up the Maritime Overseas people one day explaining that I was going to go to a job interview and they told me I'd might as well stay away from there because it was very foolish of me to come into their offices and behave the way that I did. None of which was is in my mind as to what I did except they said you're really finished with us, goodbye. Well I phoned Sally and she and her mother told me that instead of staying at the hotel, why not come and live in their apartment in Flatbush, Brooklyn.

What a mess! Sally was going to have a baby any day, her mother and I drinking alcoholically, and no income. Within two days of my arrival, Sally awoke one morning and said she saw a little boy angel up on the ceiling and told me that she believed she was ready to have the child. I took her to King's County hospital because there was no money and they deliver children at no charge. Sure enough, Sally had the little boy that we had planned on and named him after his hero grandfather, William. We brought the child home to live in the apartment with us and things were so bad money-wise that there wasn't a bassinet for the child. Little William was sleeping in a dresser drawer with a bit of fluff we arranged for the child and I went about my business of trying to get money for food, drink, and cigarettes via the panhandling route. Although I was able to keep the wife and children out of my mind, I had thoughts of my mother in that cabin in Spring Valley, New York. I went to visit her one evening and I was drinking as usual with a bit of snow around to make things more difficult. When I arrived in town of Spring Valley, I ran out of gas and was obliged by the town police to remain in the car while they got me gas for the car and put up a flare so no other cars would hit me. I got to my mother's cabin and there was no answer when I knocked at the door, and when I got back to Brooklyn I had again ran out of gas whereby the city police, their patrol cars were able to push me along the streets until they found a place for me to park the car. I think it's remarkable that I went through all of these incidents for the day, with the police helping me and me being completely drunk during every occurrence.

I had a long term goal which is nonsensical but I decided to never work again; believing that anybody could get through life by working, the secret is to get through life without working. Sally and myself (and the child) were grateful that the child was being breast-fed because there was no money for foodstuffs for the child; my panhandling money bringing in just enough for drinks, foodstuffs, and cigarettes for myself. The only source of income was Sally's mother who was working as a housekeeper. Not only providing us some moneys, but foodstuffs she was able to get from the household she was working for. One day we got a telephone call from the employers of Sally's mother who requested that I come over to their house and pick her up because she was lying on the couch dead drunk. I brought Sally's mother back to the apartment and realized that there's got to be some other way of handling this situation; not knowing about city services that may supply us with foodstuffs I believe that there's no such thing as illegitimate children, only illegitimate parents. Sally's mother not understanding this wished that Sally and I would marry; not withstanding the fact that my wife and I were only legally separated and it wasn't within the law for me to marry Sally. Instead of writing Sally's mother each time please put the words Nora, which was her Irish name from the other side. Nora insisted that Sally and I go somewhere and get married for the child's sake, which I was quite reluctant to do. Since I wouldn't cooperate, Nora went about the task of trying to make my life miserable; Sally wasn't even attempting to interfere with her mother's obscure behavior either. I was able to get a job doing porter work in a fairly upscale building in Brooklyn, New York, working from 8 am to 6 pm six days a week. I never understood where Nora got the money to be drinking at all times, but she was able to sleep all day and wait for me to come home from work at about 7 pm, and then tear into me all night long physically and verbally where I wasn't able to get any real rest. Then I had to be at work at 8 am and Nora would go to sleep for the day, awaiting my arrival for another attack towards me.

An interesting story on that porter work is that there was one of the tenants who would ring the bell almost every half hour, whereby I would have to take the freight elevator up to her back door of the apartment and pick up trash, as usual she handed me a bunch of grapes as a gift and I told her what she could do with her grapes and I was reported to the manager of the building who retired me from the position. The business with Sally's mother keeping me awake I wound up in the laundry room of the building and had laid down on the floor and fallen asleep. One of the maids came in to do the laundry and found this person (me) lying, which she reported as a dead man on the floor, causing all types of commotion and leading me to termination of the porter job. On another occasion when Nora was drunk she insisted on holding the baby and I was trying to persuade her to leave the child be because he might drop from her hands, and she got away with holding the child who did fall out of her hands and hit his head on a marble table, Nora in a drunken stupor said "Well I guess he's dead!" I didn't believe so and in case there was a question of life or not I went through my Catholic training and baptized the child myself in the sink and the child revived and that was one incident of dealing with Nora's drinking problem. I might add information concerning guilt and shame is that a simple example would be I took some money and I'm a bad person, that would be guilt whereas if I said I took some money and I did something bad, that's shame. Which by the way is much easier to deal with than guilt.

Subconsciously I must've been dealing with guilt and not being able to express it in any other way except trying to get to a semiconscious state with the alcohol. At that point in time I didn't realize that I wasn't a bad person, only someone who did something extremely upsetting to my family. I wouldn't allow myself to think of what they must've been going through with this abandonment factor of the husband disappearing and of course it would be with the children, a father's disappearance. A reflection on working with the landscaper, a fellow I was working with was a former patient at a mental hospital in New Jersey and he claimed that because of a bad knee he couldn't drive the landscaping truck between jobs, making me do the driving, which is a bit rough because it's about the one time you'd get to rest during the day; sitting in the truck between the jobs. The owner was telling me one day that the fellow in question would go to a bar every night and drink beer until he was dead drunk and then go sleep in the landscape truck, and the owner also added that he'd rather be dead than live like that and I agreed. What he didn't know and what I was doing is going back to my car every night and drinking wine until I passed out and slept in the car. Some of this book is out of time sequence because of about close to half a century of memories and conditions, however it appears that whatever did happen, I wound up on the Bowery living life as an unemployable derelict, living in cheap flops and drinking with bottle gangs and panhandling to get my next bottle of wine.

The one thing I did know about Alcoholics Anonymous, a twelve step program for alcoholism recovery, is that you got free coffee and cake at the meeting. I thought that I might go to the meeting, get some free coffee and cake, and possibly panhandle some drinking money. Since I had no intention to stop drinking it was a nice feeling to hear that if I didn't to stop I had a place that would help me, and when they say that you stop at one day at a time I thought that was great. I wouldn't drink for one day and have a barrel of Muscatel wine tomorrow. Possibly to jump ahead because I now have a barrel of muscatel wine that has been aging for about forty-one years and if I do break out and drink again it's going to be some party; all cordially invited. For anybody with road rage problems this might be my thought when I would be driving my car, anybody going faster than me was a maniac and anybody going slower than me was an idiot. I wonder how many people realize that the opposite of love isn't hate, it's indifference. Considering the time lapse and trying to pull this together, I believe that I was finally able to get myself a job with the National Distiller's Company and I was the label buyer. The fellow that was to train me was at the desk for two weeks with me and then went on vacation, leaving me in charge of all the label purchases for the holiday bottling season. An interesting side thought on alcohol is that National Distillers had two plants going 24 hours a day to keep up with demands. Also interesting and this concern is that for the cost for a quart of alcohol production-wise was a quarter; the balance being for packaging, labeling, distribution, advertising, taxes, and payroll.

Since economics was my college major, I had special training and experience in volume purchases it wasn't too difficult for me to adapt to this type of material. I was handling the process fairly well but there were certain labels that I couldn't approve because of differences in the makeup of the standard comparison label with the new production labels. I made notes on end labels that seemed to be an error on the boss's desk pending his return from vacation with questions and notes as to his approval for continued production and use on packaging of the bottles. I should've suspected something about the fellow I was working for because the other employees told me that when you're talking to the boss in the morning keep it to very few words if you can and in the afternoon try not to talk to him at all. That made me wonder as to what I've gotten myself into. It was soon enough that I found out he was a martini drinking tiger and was very difficult to work with, having had four different assistants in the last two years. An interesting thought on this deal also is that the company made a bourbon by the name of "Old Crow," with a problem of sales because of the label the powers to be came to let us know. We tried putting the crow on the different parts of the label, we tried changing the crow's image including putting the crow in a tuxedo, but the bourbon just wouldn't sell.

We tried to compete with Canadian Club by making a label that was similar to Canadian Club's but it was called Canadian Mist, so anybody trying to put that drink in someone's glass in a bar wouldn't really notice that they're not getting Canadian Club, they're getting a substitute product. I found that this was getting to be too much to live with, the constant badgering and being told by my boss that I didn't know what I was doing, made me decide to go look for another position. I had gotten a great opportunity to be a purchasing person with a great organization. I had sobriety now and I wasn't too interested in jobs with stress; but my first interview when I got to the new organization they said they had a senior and junior buyer position and with my background I was there to be a senior buyer. I actually wanted a junior buyer position because I was now kind of trying to take life easy and let the rest of the world go by but with my personality, character, etc. I said of course, senior buyer, and I was letting myself in for the stress again. I had been interviewed by several people at the organization I was interested in and the director of the company wanted to interview me and they'd let me know after that interview and for me to be there at 5 pm the next day for the interview. I told them I'd make it somehow. I told my boss as the National Distillers that I would be leaving at about 4:30 to go on some personal business and he said he guess he could spare me the half hour, but I would have to cut my lunch hour down to half an hour. This may give you an idea of the type of person I was working for and why I so much wanted to change jobs.

Well, I went through the interview with the director and it seemed to be going well, however the director said to one of the assistants "Have you checked with this steamship company he was once associated with?" As a little aside on this, when I was with Pan Am, I would come in early to the company so I could sober up by 9 o'clock because I had been drinking early in the morning and the executives would walk through the office and see me sitting there, and the assistant to the director of the new company said "Oh I didn't go back that far because I checked with Pan Am and they said when they came in they'd find Vincent there, so I suppose that's the type of person we want for our company." Whew! What a break that was for me because I wasn't sure I'd get any type of good rating from the firm that let me go after eighteen years of great service. Well I got the job and I went to National Distillers the next morning, I was there at 9 o'clock, and the fellow who told me about the half hour for lunch if he's going to let me go at 4:30, said to me, "You know Vincent, I kind of gave you a break by letting you out of this office at 4:30 but this isn't the kind of time factor we tolerate at National Distillers and I hope it won't happen again." I told him I didn't believe it would ever happen again knowing in my mind that I was going to quit. I could have said something about a song that has words to the effect of take this job and shove it, but I wasn't that kind of person and I said to myself I know I'll be leaving and I'll give just enough service so they're not left high and dry by my end.

Chapter 13

A thought on the possibility of alcoholism being a type of insanity according to the second step of AA, which states, "The key is to believe a power greater than ourselves can restore us to sanity." It's also connected with mental health in a sense because the symptoms are about the same for mental instability and alcoholism. Call it mental instability if you wish. I believe that insanity which is a description of alcoholism in a sense because it is doing the same thing over and over again expecting the same result. There's a story about this compulsive gambler in a movie theater watching a horse race on the screen and he says to the fellow next to him, "I bet you twenty dollars number five wins." and the fellow says "I'll take that bet." and number five loses, the gambler says, "Darn, I can't believe it. This is the second time it happened." The fellow says "What do you mean the second time? You mean you've seen this before?" and the gambler says, "Yes, I did, but this time, I thought he would win."

I believe this belongs in the book as I just remembered at one point I was trying to get my life together, but still drinking I took an evening job at a chain of hamburger places called "Big Daddy", basically to get money to drink, because I'd been working at Bohack's from 8 to 5 every day and would get out to this second job at 6 and work until about 2 in the morning cleaning up tables and basic kitchen work. I don't know if I was getting ahead of the game because I took running out to my car to get some of the wine from under the seat and drinking that while I was trying to do the work for the company. One night, a couple of the employees asked me if I would give them a ride home and I obliged. I was about four blocks from the store on a main highway in Brooklyn going towards their house and I ran out of gas. Whereby I asked the men if they could kindly push my car along until we found a gasoline station and they wound up outside the car pushing it along this thoroughfare wondering how could this be that he's supposed to be giving us a ride home and we're pushing his car. I recall at that time I didn't have insurance on the car and my license plates were expired so basically the fellas should have pushed me into a used car lot where I could sell the car (which eventually I did) and let me go to the Bowery, which was my real destination whether I liked it or not. The owner, Big Daddy, has pictures of himself with all celebrities put on the walls of all of his chain stores that he had, and I suspected that it was because he was donating/giving money to the celebrities and Big Daddy always had a big smile in these pictures, but in person there was no smiling about the face of Big Daddy. He told us employees that if we wished we might be able to get a hot dog or burger but to lay off any kind of roast beef sandwiches because of the extra cost in having employees dig into the pricey products.

Chapter 14

Well there I was with my diploma from Rutgers University and also deciding to go to John Jay college in the evenings to get the necessary education for certification by NY state as an alcoholism counselor. During the day I believe I was taking some type of extra Braille lessons at the blind organization and evenings at John Jay, which eventually I was able to accomplish and found that I now had all the basic necessities for certification. In the division of alcoholism in Albany which incidentally from my previous statement on insanity, division was under the department of mental health in the state of NY. However, I could not get employment. It didn't matter how much effort I put into getting interviews and getting assistance from a friend of mine who was an alcoholic in AA, who had his own employment agency and beginning to get frustrated because there was a stigma to alcoholism, and there's a stigma to visual impairment no matter what the laws might state.

I was almost ready to go back to the mop and broom factory to keep myself occupied, but I persevered and the result was a decision to go to the EPRA School for alcoholics, EPRA being Employment Program for Recovered Alcoholics. In fact they used the past tense of recovered to show that the employers would think that the alcoholic has no more problems with alcoholism, although the American Medical Association has declared it as an incurable disease, so that one would ever know when one would go back to the drink. I recall the job developer saying to the intake person at the school, something to the effect that "I have enough problems trying to get interviews for the students who are just alcoholics and now I've got to try to get one not only for an alcoholic, but one who's blind?" However I went through the school hoping that they would find something in my line and believing that if I have a desk, a phone, a chair for a client and a chair for myself, I could do the job as well as anybody else, including the background and experience of being of alcoholic. Although the school doesn't teach any particular skills, the staff tries to get the individual to have self-esteem and to go through all the type of interviews that they might get when they go out for a job or something of that nature. I handled all of this as best as I could and finally graduated, but no job.

A sidebar to this, which had no effect on my employment because I became friends with the director of the school, and one day he told me that his nephew was an alcoholic and of course the director was a recovering alcoholic himself, but the nephew was so bad he was in King's County Hospital and asked if I'd go there and speak with, which I did. Speaking about one hour's time with the fellow who was basically out of it, as I recall. He was kind of just staring into space and I was talking to him about recovery and mentioned that I would help him when he was out of the hospital, so I left and let it go at that. The director was so grateful for my help that he was able to get me an interview with the Mayor's office as a trainee at their Bureau of Alcoholism, which he drove me personally to the interview, and I was accepted as a trial for ninety days. I was so grateful for this opportunity that I became a workaholic and instead of having it as a 9-5 position, I made it a 24 hour a day thing where I met with the families of the alcoholics, I met with the employers, helped them to get employment, helped them with housing, and other benefits that they were entitled to and they seemed to have come along so well that their significant others and the alcoholics themselves were sending letters to the Mayor about how good a worker I was at assisting them at getting a new chance at life. In fact I also used to take people to Al-Anon meetings and take their significant others to Al-Anon meetings, and I guess it paid off because the time came when the Mayor was opening up a satellite office in Queens, NY, and I was appointed director. If I wrote a script for the type of position I would like to have, I could not have written anything better than the way this presented itself; a private office with a staff in Forest Hills, one of the better parts of Queens, and working next to the Mayor's office of volunteers, and having nobody to answer to, except once a month, I'd send in a report to the city.

I would get into the office at about 10:30 in the morning and go to lunch at about 12, return the next hour, and leave at 3 o'clock. No one to tell me about the time, and days off whenever I wished, and it then was the position that I looked forward to everyday, plus I was helping those who needed the help (including myself.) I was employed for about seventeen years, working for two mayors when Mayor Giuliani decided to close me up for financial purposes; I was once again out in the streets. The Mayor said that I should remove everything from my desk by Friday, because as of the following Monday, the office would be closed. Coincidentally, the legislature in Albany approved my proposal for funding to help the blind alcoholics (my research came up with 20,000 visually impaired alcoholics in the state of NY alone and nothing being done for any of them.) The money was to teach the blind to become alcoholism counselors whether they, themselves had a problem with alcohol or not, and I was to put together all of the details for the legislature for all of the allocation of the funds. I then went to work in an office on Manhattan where I was making up the details as to what is needed and how much money might be needed for each section of training, such as number of instructors that would be required and the available literature in forms such as Braille, cassette tapes, etc, etc. It was quite a project; working together with the NY state commission for the blind and the national council on alcoholism.

Where they tried to make it a federal project and I tried to keep it simple, but it was stressful because I had to be there at 9 am and leave at 5 pm daily, and be aware that I had to answer to the two authorities that were working with me. I tried to keep the program simple, but the complications that were thrown at me every day about their ways of handling the new program that I was trying to initiate were getting me upset, everyday by five I was glad to leave and by Friday night I was relieved to have two days off, but knowing that Monday coming starts the whole thing over again. If this pilot program worked in New York, it was then going to be considered for nationwide development. It would be one of the greatest advances since the creation of Alcoholics Anonymous. Meanwhile, I helped get a program together for the blind alcoholics in the five boroughs because the funds weren't coming through year after year when I was with the Mayor and we got a nice little place in Manhattan in the housing for the blind building, and they let us have a conference room where we met every Wednesday night from 6:30 until 8:30. We put out fliers and advertised the best we could to get people coming to the meetings who were blind, but leave it to the bureaucracy, the government wouldn't let us leave it only for the blind, it had to be for the handicapped of all types, so we have a meeting now for the blind, but they have other areas of illnesses there at the same meeting. And of course AA being AA, all are invited. It's part of what I tried to say about the stigma of alcoholism and blindness, that I was involved with the ADA which is the Americans with Disabilities Act and it was approved, however, with all the litigation that went on after that, I believe the initials that should represent this should be "attorney's dreams answered."

It must have been a shock to the director of the office in Manhattan where I was working because one Monday morning, I phoned her and said, "I will no longer be coming into the office, if you wish I will continue the outline necessary at my home." She was shocked and said, "Do you realize the opportunity that you're getting over here? That you're getting to be in charge of the entire operation? And you will not be getting a paycheck unless you come into office." Well, then I said "Well then I will work without a paycheck. I will finish the outline and when all the information is ready, I will bring it into the office and then we will take it from there." What a relief that was for me to say that and I did finish the project at my own living space and frankly never went back, believing that if someone else wishes to finish it and work at it, well then, more power to them. Meanwhile I got involved with a private practice, I took all my experience, education, diplomas, and certificates and put them on my wall in the living room and made a nice little business for myself as a private therapist with an interesting income, which is something within reach of most people considering that I paid fairly big money myself when I went through therapy as part of the qualifications necessary for getting into the field where they feel that you should be getting rid of your own defects and shortcomings, one way or another, so that there will be no transference which are little bit technical words for simply being don't let the defects of the person you're helping get onto you and don't let any of those shortcomings you have rub off onto the client.

When I was connected with the Mayor, I found that many people wanted psychologists or psychiatrists to help them and I'd heard of those services, but they would charge hundreds of dollars an hour and weren't really that versed in addictions. I mentioned to the clients that came to the Mayor's office that I could do the same as professionals at a lower fee and I started off at $10 a session after the Mayor's work had finished, using the political facilities. As the people were getting better, I was raising the fee until it stabilized at $35 an hour, and a half session with the opportunity to phone me 24 hours a day at my private office. As word of mouth got around to my ability to help others, I was getting more and more clients, but they were all so more emotional than addicted and I used my college psychology, plus any of my educations surrounding that area to assist them; and it's hard getting better. One client was deeply emotional and if I didn't open the door in the first fifteen seconds of ringing the bell, he would start kicking the door, also finding that he was always looking at himself in the mirror, even when he took me out to lunch or dinner with his mother he would be in the bathroom and a waiter told me he noticed when he went in there that the fella sitting with you is in there just standing there looking at himself in the bathroom mirror, and even one Thanksgiving when he said he was going to treat me and his mother to Thanksgiving dinner somewhere, we were in this classy facility and he started to argue with his mother and he jumped on the chair and started to wave his napkin in the air which was rather unsocial, I would say.

Once he came to my place dressed only in underwear with his outside clothing under his arm expecting me to figure out why he was using that behavior as a way of life. I truly believe that to be a good therapist or anyone working in the mental health field, the only four requirements are use your head, your heart, life experiences, and conscience. Although I joined the New York Federation of Alcohol counselors, and understand how important it is for the client to pay the fee, I still feel extremely awkward asking for the money as the client is leaving the session, I do believe that if you're paying for services, you should give the fee without being asked. Still, all in all, I do the same work as the Park Ave. professionals and charge about a third of their fee and have successes without any true failures, batting one thousand and you wonder why I am batting that average because nobody is to be batting one thousand! One interesting case was a lady who was a lawyer, Jewish by faith, working for the government and was married to an Algerian Muslim who was an alcoholic and wasn't working, relied on his wife for money to drink and still living in her condo where she paid all the expenses, even him using her automobile during the day which was to be a car service, but was driving only to a bar where he'd drink all day with his friends, and come home during the night causing all types of commotion in his upscale condo. She even taught him English where as when he came from Algeria, he couldn't speak English, which I believe was rather positive of the lady lawyer, and for some reason was trying to get him some type of help and would come to my office, the two of them weekly and it developed where he wanted only to drink and live off of her money. She was the perfect example of enabling, which shows that even with all of that education, professionalism, and connections to the political scene, she was unable to understand his issues.

At that time they were coming to my private office in Brooklyn and she received an appointment as Assistant Regional Attorney for the state of NY, but was required to live in Buffalo, NY. He didn't want to live in Buffalo, basically because he knew all of his drinking people were here in Brooklyn. She left without him, leaving him only her automobile, selling her condo and getting a divorce. The ex-husband would come on his own now into my office, and as we talked and I helped him in ways that I had contacts, eventually, he went on his way and no longer comes to my place, and hopefully a stronger person for the experience.

To lighten up a bit, there's a person who does sick cartoons, and one of them, of course it is a cover of a book, it illustrates a group of people on horseback in the desert sand and there's a wheelchair with a broken wheel and one person says to the other "I think we've got him now, he won't get far on foot." I had my thoughts on one, but I never illustrated it. It shows two opposing football teams, and on one side there's a fellow with a cast on his leg and he's on crutches and he's ready for kicking a field goal, and the caption shows one fellow saying to the other, "I don't think he's going to make the field goal, the wind is against him." Back to business, I had one client that was coming to my office when I was with the mayor, the director's secretary said that the fellow she brought in was her ex-husband and he was a short fellow with a coat up to his mouth but with a collar and a scarf and all that, and basically all you could see was the face and she said to her husband "This man here is a doctor, go talk to him, he'll straighten you out in fact, he's won two noble prizes but he's too humble to pick them up and I won't bother you, go into his office and talk." So he comes into my place and sits down and I'm talking to him and she's outside and for some reason. The ex-husband calls his former wife a whore and then the door swings open, she rushes in and grabs him by the neck and yells, "Who are you calling a whore?!" like she wasn't listening outside.

I gave that fellow about three hundred dollars worth of services, including talking on the telephone for several hours at any time he wished to speak to me, complaining a lot about his former wife and other areas of challenges that were troubling him. Eventually I said, "You know it's time I think you should think about settling the fee which comes to about three hundred dollars." and he replied, "Three hundred dollars! You're not worth three hundred dollars, I'll send you what you're worth." I got in the mail a check for thirty dollars. Well, we live and learn but I was grateful to have thirty dollars, which is better than no money at all. An interesting thought as to when I was living in my car in NJ, in Bergen Park where I would get up in the morning and envy everyone that was going somewhere to work, and I couldn't wait for the weekend when they wouldn't be working, so the weekend would come and then these same people would be in Bergen Park having a lot of fun, enjoying the facilities of the park and I'm sitting there thinking "This is making me feel worse because they're enjoying the fruits of their labor and I have no direction except trying to get myself my next drink." Eventually I wound up at the 23rd Street Clubhouse in New York, which is basically open from 10 am to midnight everyday, seven days a week of the year. There were AA meetings there everyday of the week, and I liked the idea of it being another home for me other than the apartment I was sharing with Sally and her mother several blocks from the clubhouse. It had some drawbacks as to disturbing the peacefulness of the place due to the various visits from the police dept by disturbances from the recovering alcoholics which I believe many of them came directly from the Riker's Island Prison to the clubhouse. I sense that when they were released the warden said here's where you may go if you want a place to stay during the day and gave the name of the clubhouse. The background of some of them included bank robbers, house burglars, forgers, and car thieves, etc. I always felt that if you wanted to get your own death certificate, there would be somebody there who would certainly make one for you which could be completely undetectable and good for legal purposes.

Knock, knock—who's there? Opportunity! To retrace a bit I recall when Sally and her mother purchased a small house in Brooklyn, I went along with them, and was sober in AA and doing a good job in my new career. Sally's mother was still drinking and put in a regulation for me that I wasn't to enter the house in the evening from my AA meeting, unless I phoned and got her permission, which was a bit of awkwardness because I was an adult now trying to get back into some kind of semblance of normalcy but yet playing by rules that made no apparent sense to me. An interesting anecdote on a fellow that I was helping to get to the AA program and we went to Brighton Beach together one day and I was going to the bathroom which was located on the beach, a bit of a house they had there and I thought well let me go into this little building and go to the bathroom; not realizing that it wasn't a straight walk to the toilet area, there were steps going down and I started falling down those steps until I reached the bottom, as I was trying to get my balance I found somebody there that I grabbed onto at the bottom and put my arms around the fellow to break my fall. The fellow that I held onto started yelling for the police; here I was a legally blind fellow who had my fall broken by another blind fellow who thought he was being mugged. The only real damage I sustained was a right toe nail and toe that was a bit out of whack which necessitated me to eventually go to Kings County clinic to have it treated.

The physician assigned to me was the director of podiatry for the hospital. During the months of the term visits until the toe was healed I received notice from the doctor that he had a private practice dealing with podiatry and had an assistant who made prosthetics, and although the person was a genius at his trade and the doctor didn't wish to lose him but the person was an alcoholic. Other than those circumstances, I found a doctor to be a very compassionate person who sincerely cared about helping the person who had a wife and a child and didn't want him to go further down then he was, even though he did appreciate the fact that there wasn't a better prosthesis maker in the business than his associate. I have since learned how complicated and technical the making of these prosthetics are and how much difficulty there must be in paying attention to all the details when you're drunk. It was similar to myself trying to do portraits at a time when I basically could hardly make out the canvas, let alone the details of the face itself that I was trying to copy. So the fellow came to my office once a week and I took him to AA meetings and general counseling about life in sobriety, if he so wished and I didn't charge a fee to the fellow although he believed it was a free service, however the doctor was to pay my fee without the assistant knowing anything about it.

The fellow's wife came to visit me once and explained to me all the trouble she was having with him as far as his drinking were concerned and the wife's insistence that the child not be in the car with the husband whenever he was driving because she couldn't be sure whether he'd be drinking that day or not and possibly causing serious trouble for not only himself but the child. In that sense I recall in my days when I was drinking I very rarely ever got into the car without drinking and I know when I first had an idea that I had to keep the drink or situation hidden from the entire family because I had my youngest daughter in the car to take to different areas like school outside activities and piano lessons, etc. Every time I got in the car with her I would take out a bottle from under the front seat which was in a paper bag and have a few good swigs before we started to go to our destination. One day I had the wife and all the children in the car together with this precocious little daughter of mine and before I started the car she said aloud "Aren't you going to drink from that paper bag before you start?" her figuring that was how you start the car, that you take something from the bottle and then you drink it and then the car starts, her not knowing anything about the ignition system. It's a form of insanity to have a high priced automobile which I would take to a liquor store and get half a dozen bottles of wine and then stop at a gas station and get one half gallon of gas.

I might call the doctor's assistant "Jack" and Jack had in the time he was seeing me gotten three cars completely demolished by his drunken driving and he wound up in the intensive care unit of the hospital three times and yet had not gotten the message that he couldn't drive safely and drink. Jack himself had one leg removed below the knee when he was twelve years old and his own problems is with the challenge of getting mobility. A side thought on that comment Jack believed he was getting my counseling at no charge, he was willing to do anything around my apartment that I asked him, that included all electrical sockets and window problems and put them fairly well in order. As time progressed, I became good personal friends with the medical doctor and he was trying to help me in other areas of my medical needs as well, which were his capability. I truly believe that sobriety isn't the absence of conflict, but the ability to cope. If you examine that you find that no matter how many situations arise when you're able to deal with them and you get them settled, at times there are others ready to take their place. Coping doesn't necessarily mean solving, but dealing with the situation and you'll notice I don't use the word problem because I feel that in this life especially in sobriety there are no longer problems, but there are situations or challenges for growth. In sobriety I did a lot of furnished room type living and one time I was told that I must leave the furnished by Saturday of the week because I asked the pastor of my catholic church if he had any idea of what might be available for my living needs.

I was now getting closer to the church than I had ever been in years, if not my lifetime. The pastor of the church told me that we should pray about this and this was on a Wednesday of the same week I was to leave because the house had been sold by the owner; and I thought myself to pray—how about someone with a room for me! That Saturday I asked the pastor had he any solution to the living conditions for me and his reply was the following, "Vincent, we have an empty convent since the nuns had decided to leave the order and also no new nuns were coming in, so you might live in that convent and here are the keys." A remarkable answer to prayer, Saturday morning I had no place to live, and Saturday afternoon I had forty rooms and baths and the pastor wanted no type of money for it, just enjoy where you are Vincent, and any finances you may wish to turn towards my direction, please give it to the poor he said. I had a professional kitchen and a dining room that was fit for a banquet, lived in by Henry VIII for the enormity of the room. A side bar on this situation is that when I was a child in Pennsylvania I would pick violets for a little statue that my grandmother had of the blessed mother and it was my joy to do so, and when I walked into this convent I could almost hear Mary say to me "Thank you for the violets."

Since my living in the convent wasn't approved by the diocese, the pastor told me it would be better if I didn't discuss the arrangement with anyone, not even to any of the other clergy in the church. Incidentally, the pastor was quite the tennis professional and had twenty-five trophies in his quarters in the rectory all for tennis and he had a choice at one time of being a tennis professional or the religious vocation and he went with the priesthood. I still wish to develop my spiritual life and decided that I might become a deacon in the Catholic Church, which required years of instruction in the evening and this position would be in addition to any work you did to sustain yourself. The pastor of the church sponsored me and I went for about six years of predeaconate studies, prior to entering the seminary and this included theology apologetics, etc. Eventually when I was to be admitted to the deaconate seminary I was refused because of my vision. I even went to the Bishop to have him override any seminary rulings that would permit me to get the education needed for deaconate services and the Bishop said to me let's leave it as god's will for you, and I wondered is this what I came for god's will for me, of course god's will for me but can't you do something and it ended with me leaving without any approval.

Anecdotal-wise to when I was with Bohacks and I was on a cash register and had still been drinking and I was running with my dog in Prospect Park, and I tripped and fell flat on my face. I was quite a mess with scrapes and cuts and I went home and put bandages and such wherever I could and left it at that. Since I didn't want Bohacks to even suspect I was drinking I made up this story about two men coming up to me and threw me to the ground and the other man started kicking me and that's how this business with my face came to be. Well, every woman that came through my register would gasp and asked "What happened?" I'd explain about those two men and the match and the cigarette etc. I must've said that to about sixty women during the day before I got a little break and I could rest. This is a good example of someone who's lying so very many times others will believe it, and I too began to believe my own lie, because as I was sort of reminiscing on the matter for some reason I said to myself "I'd like to get my hands on those two guys." Then I had to laugh because I said to myself "What two guys?" You believed your own story." A side thought on that too is that the second day of the cakes that were marked down at half price for the customers were thrown out at night in the garbage room and we employees weren't allowed to take them home, so I would put string around them and put them in the corner of the garbage room and when the pickup men came with their truck in the morning, I would tell the driver that I had about ten fairly edible cakes there in the box and suggested as to whether he would take them back to garage and share them, or his family and friends could eat them. At the time I didn't know how much garbage men were connected with the mob and were making big money and weren't very interested in some baked goods that meant absolutely nothing to a person who might be making a thousand dollars a week.

Although I didn't use the fact that I had learned many ways that a cashier could make extra money with no real way of getting caught and I still had them as possible handbook for cashiers some day, if this book doesn't sell, maybe I'll make some money on the other book but it's against my standards and I didn't use them myself and I don't believe I should share that kind of inside information with anyone else.

I had a lady client that was obsessed with sex and when she was talking to me about how many men come on to her, I was thinking to myself that I hope she wasn't thinking I wanted a relationship with her. For example, one client would come to my office and immediately start in with something such as this: "I've been sleeping with about ten different men and they have their own notions about me and what I would be to them, but one day I got home from my job and there was a message on the machine from one of the men I was having sex with such as "you have possibly given me gonorrhea", which is in a sense called in urban lingo, "the clap." She carried on so much to me about that fellow, I never date anyone with the clap, they may have gotten some other disability from me but not the clap because I'm examined by a doctor on a regular basis, and I have no sexually transmitted diseases, so that's one less I have to deal with. I mentioned to her whether or not she was concerned with attracting such diseases as HIV or AIDS. She told me she knew these men and could tell whether or not they were disease-free by looking in their eyes—their eyes of all places.

Then there was a twenty-five year old lady who was having a problem with the drink and her father would bring her into my office and the girl said that she was a tour guide on interstate buses between Florida and New York, and as it turned out to be that one day she had gotten so drunk in her hotel room over night that she wrecked the room and missed the bus that took off without her in the morning and the hotel manager said that they were holding her there and needed $2000 from the father before they'd release and let her go on her way. She was married to a fellow twice her age, just to get some type of security to live in a Long Island housewife type of life in New York, but that turned out to be a disaster and I would see this client once a week until she apparently got herself in order. Then there was the postal worker that was so angry with his superiors that he was going to blow up the post office and I had to convince him every week that he came to me that wasn't a solution to anything and to control his drinking and hopefully his anger, and we'd see what developed and that was another fellow who became responsible and is doing his best work as a postal employee. Again, there's the story of this man who's having sex with his best friend's wife and the phone rings and she answers it and hangs the phone up and says to the lover that he needn't worry because her husband wouldn't be home for some time, he's playing cards with you.

As I progressed in my chosen career of therapy, I had began to learn that the most important thing of anybody and that even includes my family, is that you can't change anyone and I use the expression such as do not try to teach a pig to fly, you only waste your time and it annoys the pig! Then there was the patient with the anger problems who was using alcohol and I suggested to him that possibly when he gets that anger issue that he'd call me or do something so considerably opposite of the anger thoughts that it might distract him until he levels off. He came to my office one day wearing a fedora hat and I commented on the hat issue in my office and his remark to me was that he'd taken the advice I had given him and when he felt that rage, instead of acting upon it, he took a razor and shaved off all of his hair and taking off the hat showed exactly that—a bald head. There was a management consultant who came to see me who had a big drinking problem, who by the way was making high income, I mentioned to him about also drastic measures and he decided to get himself a bodyguard, who would knock the drink out of his hand every time he picked one up and even went further with that because when he came into my office the next visit he had this bodyguard with him who sat in a chair several feet from him and the client said he hired this fellow on a 24-hour basis to keep him away from alcohol; another drastic measure.

Incidentally, the boy I had with Sally showed up about fifteen years ago and he came to my apartment looking for a place to stay. He had developed a drinking problem and was out of the mother's house and was out of the uncle's house, and thought that I might give him shelter of sorts. I listened to his tale of woe and after talking to him a bit I thought possibly I might help him financially to a point because he wanted money for an apartment somewhere. He came back several weeks later and said he needed money for an apartment, the same story as before, and I decided to use tough love and did not advance him any funds and didn't invite him to live in my apartment because I thought I would certainly be enabling the fellow. I gave him an out on his direction in life as to possibly help me in the field of counseling whereby I could use my contacts to get him an education and hopefully a license, and we'll head in that direction and meanwhile I pointed him to meetings of AA, which is an interesting anecdote as follows. Prior to this occasion I hadn't been with my son in approximately ten years, I was walking to my house one day and a fellow from my AA group (the clubhouse) saw me and asked if I was going to a meeting that night at the relocated clubhouse, I mentioned to him that I had a new group that I was attached to and that I would be going to the meeting tonight at my current AA group. A side thought on that is I recall when the boy was graduating elementary school, the eighth grade, in Pleasantville, New York, where he was now living with his mother and the mother invited me to his graduation. I put together an overnight bag with some clothing figuring I would stay there for the weekend, and I made it up to Pleasantville by train and I got to the apartment, and the mother looked at me and asked what I was doing with the suitcase, and I mentioned that I was there for the weekend and she told me very indignantly that I couldn't stay there for the weekend and there was a train leaving at midnight that I could get on to get back to Brooklyn. She made it certain that I was not welcome in the housing area.

There was a child there in the room when I went into the apartment and I heard this child calling Sally "Mommy" and I was curious and I said nothing at that time, but I turned around and decided to go home waiting for that train, which didn't come in at midnight, it came in at 2 am. When I got home it was about six in the morning, so it was quite a wait and I got back to my place with the curiosity as to who that child was. When I spoke to Sally on the phone, I had mentioned something about the child, which Sally at the time said she was babysitting for the people next door. I had it in my head that what child would call a stranger "mommy.' I learned from my son later on as we talked more that the mother had taken up with the Vice President of Art-Carved Diamonds where she was employed and that child was the result of that relationship. Anyway, the fellow who had asked me to come to the clubhouse meeting was at his meeting earlier that evening, I think the 6 pm meeting, and my own group was at 8:30, and going around the room saying something, the fellow said that he had met Vinny today, that's me, and everything was going well with him, etc, etc, here's where it gets a little like an Alfred Hitchcock film. I learned this all later, but after the meeting was finished a young boy came up to the fellow that commented on me and said I know this program is anonymous but you know that Vincent you mentioned, by any chance is his last name Seplesky, and the fellow was a bit shocked to hear a last name like that because they're generally not used around AA and he asked the young boy why he wanted to know, and the remark from the boy was if it's Seplesky, I'm his son. The fellow said in a state of shock, "Well, would you like to meet your father?" of course the man not knowing the circumstances, the son obliged stating it's been some time since I've been with him, and the fellow said you know I'll take you to meet him tonight, he'll be at a certain meeting because the son didn't know where I lived and he came to the meeting with the fellow and we had a reunion after all those years.

What a place to have a reunion, in a meeting of AA. That's how the boy got my address and telephone number which I gave him during the evening as we reminisced a bit and he let me know other details of a sordid lifestyle that he'd been living since his mother had gotten involved with other men, including his having to leave high school where his marks were in the top percentile of the school, he had to leave school to make a living for himself. Incidentally at one point during all this and I'm not too sure of the time frame but the son was living with Sally somewhere in Brooklyn in an apartment I was asked by Sally if I could pay the rent for her because she was up against it financially and I would have the boy meet me at the clubhouse and I would give the rent to the boy to take to his mother. The mother didn't want me to come to the apartment, I found out later that was because she was living with another fellow who wasn't working, and she didn't want me to get wise to the fact that I was paying rent for him, her, and my son and this was a little difficult out of my minimum social security check I was getting out of my visual disability at the time. Then there was a disappearance again for a while until as I had mentioned at an AA meeting. This has to be told, I was helping a fellow at the Salvation Army in Brooklyn, and was legally blind and was residing there until better quarters could be found for him. He also had an alcohol problem and I would stop by once a week to speak with him and got to know the counselor who was stationed at the Salvation Army and she was involved with helping the fellow. She was a recovering alcoholic who was doing an internship to eventually get licensed by the state, which is one of their requirements before certification is that you have some personal dealings with the alcoholic community.

As I had mentioned before I was in the coal-mining town in Pennsylvania, as I was sharing with the female counselor weekly after I visited with the fellow I would talk a bit about personal life, alcoholism, etc, she told me about her own alcoholism and related to me that she came to New York City to become a model, and an actress and had succeeded as both to a certain point, but the alcohol eventually ruined her ambition and her career. Well, anyway who's ever heard of Tamaqua and I never mentioned that to the lady but she explained to me one day that she was interested in starting an AA group in her hometown where she was raised and was talking to her mother about the project. I nearly fell off of the chair when the lady told me something her mother had said to her, and it was "Justine, who's ever heard of AA in this town, you know there aren't any drunken folk in Tamaqua." We were raised in the same town, but there was that separation from those families who owned the mines and those who worked in them, apparently her family was one of the mine owners and my grandfather was the mine worker, so there wasn't too much socializing between the two groups. Coincidence?, I think not—there are too many coincidences in the AA program for them to be acknowledged as such. There must be another answer and I believe it to be an outside source.

Spirituality wise, when I think of the method for getting sinner's to repent, the savior gave the message to twelve sinners to help them and when the time came to help the alcoholics in this world, the message was given to two drunks to begin a program to help the alcoholics, i.e. Bill Wilson and Dr. Robert Smith. I was in a church once and I was really down and out and I asked God if I might get a cigarette somewhere and as I walked out of the church, in the last pew was a full pack of cigarettes, and when I would go into the church everyday, I would see a little car in a gas station, I thought it was so cute and I did thank God for those cigarettes and I said "You know how about that car? I could use an automobile." So I asked the station owner how much he wanted for the car and this is the answer I received, "Someone just left that car here and said if anyone wants it, they can have it. You could use it yourself," the car guy said and the station owner said to me, "You know, if you want it, you can have it at no charge." Talk about over-answering from the almighty. Again, I recall when I was having a problem with my ear being clogged, I was told by the hospital that if it clogs at anytime, all I could do is put in a few drops of peroxide and it should open up for you, and I had been doing that for two weeks and it wasn't opening up and I said to my higher power, "I am going to try this once more and if it doesn't work I am going to go to the hospital for this ear." Viola! The ear opened up and I was so grateful that I said to God, "What about my toe which is giving me trouble?" So you can see how I was grateful for those few seconds. Boy I'm so happy about that and then I start asking about something else.

Eventually the boy came into my life and I was trying to help him with his alcoholism but was getting nowhere, and I asked him to go see a therapist who had helped me and he did go to his office and the therapist said to me, "You know, your son was here, but I don't know if I can do anything to help him because it's more of a physical complication." He did refer him to his partner who's more of a psychiatrist, and the psychiatrist had diagnosed my son as paranoid, psychotic, bipolar, with conditions of alcoholism and substance abuse, and had treated him with medications besides the talk therapy he had gotten from my friend. I must say this in connection with alcoholism how pertinent the anecdote pertains to our decision each time we decide to drink. This little man goes home to his little house and packs his little bag to go on a little vacation, and his little neighbor comes in and says, "What are you doing little man?" and the little man says, "I am packing my little bag to go on a little vacation." and the little neighbor says, "Don't you think you should say you're going on a little vacation God willing?" and the little man says, "I am going on a little vacation." and lightning flashes and boom! The little man turns into a little frog. The little man spends the next seven years living in a swamp with all of the other little frogs and all the slime and ooze and gook eating bugs. After those seven years he turns into a little man again, so the little mean goes back to his little house and thinks now I am going to go on a little vacation and little neighbor comes in and asks, "What are you doing little man?" and the little man says, again, "I am packing my little bag to go on a little vacation." and the little neighbor says, "Don't you think you should say you're going on a little vacation God willing?" Do you think that the little man is going to take a chance living another seven years in a swamp or is he going to use the phrase God willing?

In a sense as alcoholics we're choosing in one sense to say I'll live in the swamp with all of the nonsense that goes along with that. I was sitting in the clubhouse one day and there was a lady on the phone and she was distraught and had been drinking and she said she was going to kill herself because no one wanted her and no one loved her, and I said "Wait a minute, let me come out there and talk to you" and the woman said, "I haven't eaten in two weeks" and I said, "Well, I'll bring you some food." So I stopped at a place near her house and I picked up some food to bring to her. It was a bit of a problem to get to he even though she had given me her address and subway directions and when I got out of the subway, the snow had gotten deeper and I got to her house and a rather swanky place I must say, a rather ritzy apartment from what I could make out with my limited sight, but I give her food and talk to her for several hours about sobriety and her feelings of being depressed. Some of you may recall that years passed they had a lady represent Reingold beer, and it was always narrowed down to six finalists and the pictures were displayed in various places where beer was sold, bars and stores, and you had to vote by checking off a name on a little ballot box and eventually they would count up the ballots nationwide and they would name Miss Reingold for the year. That entailed different settings for the season where they had Miss Reingold posing in summer clothes or winter clothes, but the caption was always the same "My beer is Reingold the dry beer" says Miss Reingold 1959. As I said, she had been a former Miss Reingold winner, married twice, her first husband a bad marriage for whatever reason and her second husband, an alcoholic who was always hiding out in a veterans administration detox unit at the veterans hospital whenever he got too sick to drink. I got to know the lady more, he might have gotten sick of her at times because of her behavior pattern particularly when she had beer or wine in her. Apparently the children she had from her first marriage wanted nothing to do with her, and her two little children were in foster homes, due to her drinking in the household.

Chapter 15

I turned to Miss Reingold and I told her I had to be leaving and she said, "You can't really leave now because of the snow conditions, and you can stay at my apartment." Apparently, at this time her husband was at the veterans unit in detox and she had her bedroom, and she had a bedroom for the children that were in the foster home and I assumed I would be sleeping in the children's room, but she insisted that I stay in the same bed as she did, and in the throes of alcoholism that she was and me trying to be Mr. Nice Guy, and not upset her, made the ultimate sacrifice of sleeping in the same bed as Miss Reingold. I remained away from her sexually in the bed and in the morning hours I went back to my house wondering what all of that was about, what I've gotten myself into, and what direction was that woman headed. As I thought through the night considering how my friends were at the AA clubhouse, trying to get their ladies at the same time as trying to get sobriety as the song goes, "If they could see me now!" I would bring Miss Reingold to the meetings at the clubhouse every Sunday and talk to her about sobriety whenever I visited her apartment and when I was in the location, she insisted that I lay in the bed with her while I was talking to her about sobriety. Then at the meetings she was all guised up looking like something out of a store window.

Miss Reingold would cook special dinners for me, I recall being there during the Christmas holiday and the children were released from the foster home to spend the holiday with their mother, and yet I was saddened to hear the children talking about wanting to return to Mrs. Maggorie's house, making the mother feel somewhat sad due to the fact that she had gotten them so many expensive gifts for the holidays. Miss Reingold was now getting sobriety and really getting in an interesting relationship and it turned out that I was soon living in the same building as she was. I had arranged with the owner that I could store all of my belongings in the basement of the building during the week of Thanksgiving. I had arranged through my contacts to have the children returned to her, because I said the lady had achieved sobriety, a place to live and the children could now return to their mother. I went up to visit her on the Wednesday before

Thanksgiving, and I was shocked because the firemen were just leaving her apartment, the fire had destroyed most of her beautiful apartment and Miss Reingold was lying there semi-conscious (just drunk) and unharmed, and I sat down next to her on the rug because there wasn't any furniture (she had to light a candle to get some light in the apartment.) Miss Reingold had decided to celebrate the return of her children with a bottle of wine and a cigarette, and of course the rest is history because she set fire to the couch and that was the beginning of everything going up in smoke and the owner walks in while I was talking to her and he says to me: "You bum, you're sitting here with that other bum and you reek of scotch, and now you set fire to my apartment, my building, and you wanted to live here, now move all of your junk out of the basement tomorrow, Thanksgiving day, or I throw it in the trash." I thought what a bad deal that was, going from having a nice apartment to getting my "junk" thrown out of the building on a holiday, Thanksgiving Day. The owner leaves and in walks Miss Reingold's brother who says, "Don't be an actress. Get up and come with me, you're going to stay at my place, you're getting out of here tonight." I'm left there with the candle in the dark, and I went back to my place figuring what the heck that was all about.

I spent Thanksgiving Day getting my belongings out of the basement the best I could and the Friday after that I went into the office and I got a phone call from Miss Reingold accusing me of deserting her. She had no idea of what had gone on and she thought that I had left her forgetting that she had left with her brother, leaving me stranded. Eventually, Miss Reingold ended up in a furnished apartment room where I visited her stepping over the empty wine bottles and beer cans just to get to a chair and be able to talk to her in her drunken haze, and as far I know, the next time I visited her building, she was gone, no one knew what had happened to her, and that was the last I had known about Miss Reingold because she never contacted me again, and I can only surmise that she had passed away. Sometimes I think that if God cannot take alcohol away from us, then he must take us away from the alcohol by removing us from the planet. An interesting thought during my drinking days in Manhattan, I would find myself sitting in a bar somewhere in Greenwich Village, at about 2 o'clock in the morning, while sitting in the bar I would read a sign at the back of the bar, which read, "My candle burns at both ends, it will not last the night, but all my foes and all my friends, gives a lovely light!" That was the way of thinking about life and yet not realizing that there would be an end to this jet set life that I was in. A quick thought about when I was with the jet-set crowd I would drink with Jackie Gleason, the comedian at Whites in Manhattan. At that time Jackie was always drinking, he wouldn't eat food, and he wore a $3000 custom made suit and his hair coiffed and face perfectly groomed and was quite attractive, and the maitre'd came over to him one day and said, "Mr. Gleason, we appreciate your patronage and do hope you will continue to come to our establishment, however, you seem to be only drinking without taking any of the food from the menu. Is there any special reason that you're not taking any meals here?" Mr. Gleason said sarcastically in a bus driver sort of voice, "Confidentially pal, I understand the food here stinks." Anyway, in connection with my new spirituality and my becoming third order Franciscan I do think that for me to become chosen to enter and official order of the Catholic church is that the holy spirit must have a sense of humor.

I had a client in Sheepshead Bay, right near the water, I would go to her apartment because she would refuse to visit me, and that's the kind of extra mile that I would go for people at times, the very first tine I went there, she was at the door with a glass of wine in her hand. When I went in, she put her arms around me and was very amorous to say the least, and I spent most of the time of that visit just trying to get her to stay calm enough to listen to something about sobriety. Subsequent visits turned out to be the same way due to her being under the influence of her wine. It turned to be that she could no longer afford my services, because she needed money to have her hair done and buy alcohol weekly. She introduced me to her daughter and son who lived in the same building, and her son was a heroine addict and I made arrangements for him to go to one of the rehabilitation centers I had a connection with at no extra charge to the fellow, in fact the rehab owner himself came to the apartment on a Sunday with his car to drive the fellow to the center. It turns out that I lost that connection because the very next day, the son slammed one of the counselors in the face, and that was the end of that.

I was having problems with my head and I went to a clinic, a friend of mine who was the father of one of my clients (a real estate person) closed up his office and was going to stay with me while I was there. The doctor had to leave the office, he asked me to come back tomorrow and my friend came back with me the next day, we had to wait for another five hours . . . and he said, "Lady, we're not coming back tomorrow or ever! Come on, Vincent, I am going to take you to Staten Island." and that's what he did, he took me to the hospital to have someone look at my head and that's where I wound up at Staten Island Hospital in 2000. After about a week of testing, they sent me to Metropolitan Jewish Geriatrics center in Borough Park, where I had four drugs put into me throughout the day where they tried to kill the infection of the skull and that went on for about six weeks before I was released. The infection of the skull had destroyed the plate that was put in during the original skull operation in 1972. The plate was removed and I had to wear a protective helmet for about a year to make sure that all the infection had left the skull, and the plate. Eventually I had a titanium plate put into the opening in the skull that's there to this day, and if anyone wants to have cable TV, just point the antennae toward my head and you have satellite TV.

The high cost of medical treatment, the entire procedure at four of those hospitals with all the doctors and all the procedures, the total cost was $400,000, $20,000 of which wasn't paid for by Medicare. All of the hospitals were willing to accept the minimum payments due monthly, except for the geriatrics center who said they wanted one check for $2,200, or it goes to collection, which it eventually did go to a collection agency, which I am still refusing to pay a place that was already paid $3000 by Medicare for the six weeks, because of their mistakes with medication. One night I got one pill in a cup and I told the nurse that should be two pills in the cup and the nurse said, "I must have given the other one to someone else. Just take this one." An Allergist that I was involved with claimed that the infection could have gone down to the brain and killed me, which is amazing because King's County Hospital was so lax in their treatment the entire time I was there. I have been involved with the Franciscan, I was a vice minister for about eighteen years and the following happened that the minister could no longer fulfill his duties, so I was placed as acting minister of the fraternity and we had a friar who was assigned to us as a spiritual assistant, as now I was minister of the Franciscan, and I phoned him to let me know my position and that I was a recovering alcoholic of AA, and his reply to me was, "Well, isn't that interesting because I am the chairman of an AA in Manhattan myself!" One of the members wanted to renew his vows, so we made arrangements because it's somewhat complicated, in that you need special approvals for a mass set and special dignitaries present as witnesses that are in the hierarchy, and I spent a considerable amount of time and the following would occur . . .

Chapter 16

Having spoken to the friar half a dozen times, I expected to be no problem with the re-profession of vows, the night of the services was scheduled and the entire fraternity of about twenty-five people were there, the alter was set up, except there was no priest. One of the members went to the friary to find out where the priest was and they found him, and he said he had no such information concerning any re-profession of vows that night, and they came back and said that out loud at the fraternity that the friar knew nothing about this and everybody was looking at me since I was in charge. I knew they were looking even though I have no sight because I could see the heads turn like "Vincent, what did you do." and I knew I did everything right and my thoughts were I bet you that friar has a drinking problem. Every time I called the friary, the next week, I was given the runaround, the friar is not here, he will be back do you want to leave a message and after a while I mentioned something to the fraternity that he might have a problem with alcohol and if doesn't remember what I was talking to him about, and they all told me to be a little more careful about what I was saying about one of their own members since we were all apart of the same Franciscan order.

About one month later, we had a fill-in friar say the mass at our third order meeting and he was the guardian of the church and he said, "We all might pray for so and so, we sent him away for rehabilitation for alcoholism and it was the same priest that I was involved with, with the re-profession of vows situation." When I was the mayor's director, I had justifiable pride in gaining that position even without vision, and after quite a struggle, I was enjoying some of the semi-celebrity status that I had. In moving in that circle I was one of the special speakers at the AA anniversary for one of the top radio talk show hosts, who wishes to remain completely anonymous. Each year you get one year of sobriety, you can have an anniversary night when you can invite your speaker to give their speech. The talk show fellow has a driver and he has the driver leave him off at a diner than walks to the AA meeting having told the driver to come back again in a couple of hours and then return to the diner where he's picked up to go home. This is so secretive, that he doesn't even want the driver to know that he's at a meeting of alcoholics anonymous. I may quote Mother Theresa, she had an interesting thought, "We do not do great things, what we should try to do is small things with great love."

The celebrant at the AA meeting, this talk show fellow had this ending. He said, "I don't like to celebrate anniversaries, the only reason I celebrate is that if there is a newcomer, walking into the rooms and sees the cake, the candles, and the decorations, he can point at me and say, "If the son-of-a-bitch can stay sober, then so can I." I learned that my oldest son, and I got this from the girlfriend who wrote me because the boy still wants nothing to do with me, she said that my son learned to play the guitar on his own and formed a little band and had put out several albums, toured England which is quite an accomplishment considering at one time I did not wish to get him guitar lessons because I thought that he would be a hippie groupie and he is now kind of out of the business and settled down with a 9-5 job, stable without his going over the edge, so to speak. I saw his picture on one of the album covers when I had sight, and his hair was still long which was one of the problems I had with the boy because I couldn't get him to cut his hair and when I saw the photo of him, I threw the album away and didn't listen to it. Interesting how things fall into place because in this section of the order I am to pay my own expenses, I get no help from the order and when I was sent to Rome at the 800th anniversary of St. Francis, I was representing the east coast of Franciscans, they sent a translator with me, but I had to pay my own airfare. I went over to the bishops office in Manhattan to get a pass to see the Pope and the fellow that worked there was the same fellow that I had gotten a job for several years back, and when he heard that I was leaving for Italy, he said, "Let me pay the airfare" so it worked out well. By the way, I never did get to visit with the Pope because at that time I was assisting the birthplace of Francis and I thought, well let me remain here because it was a four hour bus ride back to Rome, so if you find that the Pope is over here on one of his travels, he might be looking for me!

A thought on alcoholism and how it compares with the thoughts of Elizabeth Kubler Ross; where she listed the phases of dying—such as denial, anger, bargaining, despair, and acceptance, it occurs to me that those are the same five stages that a person goes through in their alcohol recovery, i.e., the first is denial of the alcoholism, the second is anger, "Why me? Why do I have to go through all of this misery?" The third comes bargaining, "God if you will get me through this, I will not do this again, if you get me through the sickness, the misery of this hangover, I'll certainly give up the drink." The fourth is despair, feeling there is no hope, feeling I can't overcome this alcoholism, this ongoing condition and there is no hope. Finally, there is acceptance of all that we know in the past and what's going to be of us now, and not so much the word acceptance, but serenity.

I recall that at one time when my wife's cousin was visiting us for the day and he was certainly a heavy drinker and even had a bottle in his pocket when he came through the door for his visit, and eventually my wife said, "How about taking him home?" I decided to give him a ride back home in one of the lower scale neighborhoods. I was a drinker at the time but I don't believe I was an alcoholic yet, and I brought him up to his apartment and inside I was shocked to find all of the walls covered with roaches and I mean so many that you could hardly see the paint on the walls, and they were all over the table, the glasses, the cups, and he offered me a drink from one of the glasses that he was pouring whisky into and I said, "No, I think I'll get by without one today." I went home, when I would visit the VP of the New York Life Insurance company in his apartment, it was a roach-town because I would be sitting on the couch talking to him and brushing the roaches off of me as I could feel them crawling because although the sight was gone, I could still feel the roach crawling. Somehow I could always sense when there were roaches even without sight because of the general ambience of the area that I was visiting. Actually when I would visit the McAllister lady, which I may have put in the book and as such be my adventures with the McAllister tugboat family and their super-wealth that I found the roaches there unbelievable even without sight again and the general sloppiness of the place, which is why I believe the balance of the family were pretty much staying to themselves, staying away from this family member.

I would clean up as best I could, however, it was always as bad the next week as it was previously because you could feel the trash underfoot on the ground, and you could feel the tables with uneaten food, dirty cups and empty bottles, and cans which were a disturbance to me, and I am sure that she did not understand what anything was about because she was on the edge. Which reminds me of a story of a roach and fellow who was in prison for twenty-five years and the only thing he accomplished in his prison time was to teach a roach to dance. When he was released from prison, he put the roach in his pocket and walked into a bar and he went in to get a drink, and he thought about how much money he was going to make with this dancing roach. He ordered a drink at the bar and the bartender when to get the drink for the man, and the man took the roach out of his pocket and placed it on the bar and said to the bartender, "Come here I want to show you something." So the bartender comes over and sees the roach and takes his bar rag and smashes down on the roach and says to the man, "I regret that this roach got in here, we usually don't have a problem with them, I'm sorry." In that sense sometimes, in life we believe willing our lives over to a higher power that the source is just waiting for us to do that and then bang! It got you! But that's not how it works!

It may have been stated in the book previously, I stayed with the McAllister woman every Saturday and Sunday night from 6 pm until 2 am at her apartment and when she wound up at nursing home finally, I stayed with her every Saturday for five years from noon until nine at night, mostly listening to her same jabbering of when she was in Hollywood and all the other nonsense in her life. I didn't do that for any of the money of the family, however, it would have been nice for them to give me one of the tugboats that were in the bottom of New York Harbor where I could have at least raised the boat somehow and slapped my name on the side and used it for it's rightful purposes. The lady knew that I was basically sightless, however she insisted on having me look at a special house across the street from where we were walking, and I could hardly see McAllister, and yet she kept insisting that I comment on that "pretty house" across the street. There's the anecdote of the farmer who had a beautiful oak tree in front of his house and he loved to sit under the shade in the summer time and admire the beautifully colored leaves in the fall, and it was one of his pleasures in life. One day he saw a squirrel climb the tree and looked into the hole and noticed the tree was hollow inside, eventually getting a tree surgeon to check the tree. The tree surgeon told the farmer, that indeed it was a hollow tree and that one day it might fall down on the house if there was a windstorm, and crush the house. "I love that tree and the tree surgeon said it would cost several hundred dollars to take that tree down safely", and as he was concerned about all of this he said to himself, "I wish I had never seen that squirrel."

The corollary to this was when I was first able to put ninety days together in AA, without a drink, I was then going out speaking at other groups sharing my story and I would go with a fellow that wore the most prestigious men slacks outfits in the city. He would be in that plant working for his father and the only job he could work at was pressing the slacks before they were all ready for shipment to the different stores. It would be embarrassing when his father would be introducing some of the company staff to people in the business that he would say, "This is so and so, and this is so and so, and this is my son, the presser." Before we went into any meeting group, he would take out a bottle from the glove compartment and take a few slugs of whiskey and replace it in the glove compartment, and I said "Isn't that strange?" and he said, "Oh no, I generally do that before I go into any meeting because I don't know how I would be able to talk to all of the drunks in there without taking a drink." I thought that was against the rules and of course it was, and I was reminded of the story of the farmer and the squirrel, and I might say the important comment was "I wish I had never seen him take that drink." Because it did bring down my ideals about what AA is about and it is parallel to what the farmer said about seeing the squirrel.

Client-wise I recall one couple that were having trouble with their son who was destroying their family in a little town in Queens. He was so upsetting that their little daughter who was going to school was concerned that the son would come to the school with his drinking and disrupt the class that she was attending. The parents with their enabling style decided to sell the house and not let the son know where they moved to and take the daughter out of the school and put her in a different school. They're the type of people that will go to any length not to face the reality of an alcoholic in the family. To be somewhat spiritual at the moment when I think of the AA program, it is to me a God given program to help the alcoholics and it is similar to when Jesus was on Earth and he wanted the message to be carried to other people as to how to live their lives and not be sinners. He gave the ideas to twelve sinners to go out and give that message and now with the message given to the entire drinking population who were alcoholics, he didn't give the program to the hierarchy, or the educators, or the scientists, he gave it to two drunks, and from there, the program grew.

Along the same lines that there is a message of why do I feel like I am at the topmost of a sailing ship in a storm? How did I get those bruises and bumps, and why do I feel like throwing up throughout the day? One might guess that it is from some alcoholism literature and it actually came from Proverbs, Chapter 23, verse 32 and onward. Of course, I paraphrased the bible reading but the point is how other things in life are similar to our dealings with alcohol and yet we try to complicate something that should basically be something simple. If you have a condition such as alcoholism, and you do not drink for a day at a time, you will have the disease under control. Every time I pass a church, I stop in for a visit, so that when they carry me in, the lord won't say, "Who is it?" That's how grateful I feel for my recovering process as an alcoholic who was one way or another the prodigal son who left home and lived in the worst conditions until he was able one day to say something to the effect that I'm going back to where I was, it was better there than it is here, but it was some process for me to hold onto all the negatives in my life before I was able to return, my family is still basically upset with my alcohol behavior and my higher power who I chose to call God who accepted me back who was waiting for me to return.

Chapter 17

I was finally back with my god, hopefully I was accepted, and the expression went through my mind with biblical teachings such as, "There is more joy in heaven over one sinner that repents than for ninety-nine that have no need for repentance." There's a fellow who I was helping who was from an Ivy league college who was having problems with life issues, he was being helped by a psychiatrist for the last ten years, not being employed since graduation from this elite college. I did my best to assist the gentleman and had some part in his turnaround in his responsible way of life, and I feel somewhat at ease with myself that I do not turn away from anyone and this fellow was a little more difficult than others to handle, my education in that area certainly was pertinent to this situation. The reader may have noticed that the book is somewhat rambling and somewhat out of sequence, but that is why I tried to keep it simple. I feel that I am talking to you as if you are sitting in my living room and we're having coffee, so I hope you'll bear with me or have borne with me through the ramblings and possibly have some identification with my experiences. As I try to conclude this memoir, I hope that others may try to experience my ideals and hopes which is summed up in the following thought that: "There are two days in every week about which we should not worry, two days which should be kept free from fear and apprehension.

One of those days is yesterday, with its mistakes, cares and sorrows. All of the money in the world cannot bring back yesterday. It cannot erase a single word we said or erase a single act we performed. Yesterday is gone.

The other day about which we should not worry is tomorrow, with its bright promise and poor performance. We have no stake in tomorrow, for it is as yet unborn. It is not the experiences of today that drive men mad, it is when we add together the burdens of those two awful eternities, the remorse or bitterness over what happened yesterday and the dread of fear of what tomorrow may bring, that we break down. This leaves us one other day and that day is today. Therefore let us live one day at a time!

The End